Appraisals: Kiriti Sengupta
Breaking the Barriers

Appraisals: Kiriti Sengupta
Breaking the Barriers

Editors
Sunil Sharma and Dustin Pickering

TRANSCENDENT ZERO PRESS

Published in the United States of America in May, 2017 by Dustin Pickering and Zachary Weiss, at Transcendent Zero Press, 16429 EL Camino Real Apt. #7, Houston, Texas 77062-5786

Email: Editor@transcendentzeropress.org
Website: www.transcendentzeropress.org

All rights reserved. No part of this publication may be reproduced or transmitted (other than for purposes of review) in any form or by any means, electronic or mechanical, including photocopy, recording, or any information storage and retrieval system without the prior permission in writing from the publisher or the copyright holders where applicable.

Cover concept & design: *Chitrangi*

ISBN-10:1-946460-94-X
ISBN-13:978-1-946460-94-3

Library of Congress Control Number: 2017942311
Copyright © individual contributors 2017

Price: US Dollars $15.00
INR: Rs.400/-

Distributed in India by hawakal.com (*Hawakal Publishers*)

Contents

Publisher's Note	9
Preface	16
An Education in Truth through Pursuit — **Dustin Pickering**	20
Epitomizing the Free Thinker — **Casey Dorman**	33
Kaleidoscopical Kiln — **Manu S Kurup**	41
Kiriti*babu*: My experience of a poet as a man — **Pranab Ghosh**	47
A Study of *The Earthen Flute* and *Reflections on Salvation* — **Dolonchampa Chakraborty**	52
Kiriti Sengupta Makes His Way to Sanskrit Literature through Indian English Poetry — **Kaushik Acharya**	59
How to Use Poetry to Drive Home the Point — **Casey Dorman**	70
Waiting in the Garden of Eden — **Dustin Pickering**	74
Dreams of the Sacred and Ephemeral — a review by **Duane Vorhees**	79

Thoughts on Reading *The Earthen Flute* and *Reflections On Salvation* —
Duane Vorhees 86

Sacred and Ephemeral — *"Vision or a waking dream?"* —
Tuhin Sanyal 90

The 'Self' is the Surveyor — an Analyst —
P C K Prem 97

Extracting the Tooth, Extracting the Truth! —
U Atreya Sarma 108

Kiriti Sengupta — a Pioneering Genius in Poetizing Yogic Science —
Dalip Kumar Khetarpal 116

The Making of a Poet —
U Atreya Sarma 125

The Reciting Pens —
a review by **Don Martin** 130

My Glass of Wine —
a review by **Eileen Register** 134

The Heady Wine of Love and Spirituality —
Shernaz Wadia 138

Not Charioted by Bacchus and his pards: Kiriti Sengupta's *My Glass of Wine* —
Rumpa Das 143

My Glass of Wine — a Trendsetting Ensemble —
Seshu Chamarty 148

Reverse Out —
Gopal Lahiri 151

Fragmented Narratives in a Stream of Consciousness —
Usha Kishore 156

A (Re)Versed World —
Soumen Jana 161

Man in the Botanical Garden: The Fallen, the Forbidden, the Golden, the Heaven-Going Tree versus the Tree Turned Upside Down —
Bishnupada Ray 170

The Reverse Tree —
a review by **Eileen Register** 174

Healing Waters Floating Lamps — Lanterns, Fireflies, and Will-o'-the-Wisps —
Vibha Malhotra 184

Journey with the Self —
Sharmila Ray 188

Direct References to Life —
Ananya S Guha 192

Acceptance of Life with its Crevices —
Saktipada Patra 195

The Premise of Language —
Ananya S Guha 200

A Mix of Mythology and Personal Meditations —
Nathan Hassall 203

The Earthen Flute —
a review by **Sunil Sharma** 207

The Tenets of Existentialism and Eternal Quietude —
Scott Thomas Outlar 211

A Stylistic Reading of [Four] Prose Poems by Kiriti Sengupta —
Susanta Kumar Bardhan 214

The Earthen Flute — A Flux of Contraries —
Tuhin Sanyal 231

A Poet in Search of Unity in Existential Disjoints —
P C K Prem   237

Not Just another Writer among the Mass —
Koushik Sen   246

Reflections on Salvation: A necessary read —
Pranab Ghosh   251

Redefining the canon — Radical art and craft of Kiriti Sengupta: Brief meditation on his book of prose poems: *Reflections on Salvation* —
Sunil Sharma   256

In Conversation with Kiriti Sengupta —
Gopal Lahiri   265

In Conversation with Kiriti Sengupta —
Dustin Pickering   271

My Husband-turned-Writer Kiriti Sengupta —
Bhaswati Sengupta   281

My beloved Kiriti*da* —
Munshi Md. Younus   283

A Letter to Kiriti Sengupta —
Bitan Chakraborty   285

The Author is Redundant —
Kiriti Sengupta   290

Notes   294-297

Biographies   298-311

Publisher's Note

The New Paradigm: Poet of Virtue

I.

This age suffers from a strange malaise. We see the politicians courting God and religion in their spectacle; we see religion ascending the throne with little humanity; we see the decadence of capitalism destroying the humanity we have let go of; and most of all, we see empty faith parading the streets as a mere moniker without the proper garb. They say the Emperor wears no clothes, and that lone person who decries the idiocy of the Emperor's display watches as the threads come apart.

We are living in a Trump age, a stirring age of restlessness and ignorance. We Americans are isolated from the world by geography and culture, and our President dons the isolationist mask because that is what we want. We may believe as thinkers that this is only an American stunt. This collection shows us strangely that the malaise disrupts all the world, not just the country named for mercy.

Kiriti Sengupta embodies the new paradigm of the poet. Today, to be a poet will inevitably make your life difficult. Asked for reasons why pursuing a craft that will not pay, you are dry. What role does the poet play? Octavio Paz and Pablo Neruda acted as ambassadors for their countries. Americans, however, are shrinking their interest in poetry. What is the poet then, now?

A poet's role now is much more important than it has been. Perhaps this explains why poets struggle and are forgotten commonly. Today's poet is a Poet of Virtue. Virtue, in the etymological sense, is strength and valor. This implies a war perhaps? Yes, the war is us against ourselves. No, not in an individual sense! In a sense collectively: we ignore our best qualities as beings and we neglect ourselves. Everyone now is a beast of some burden, often unknowing.

The Poet of Virtue is one whose valor makes us face our truth, and reminds us of how special and good our world can be. We take it for granted in the rush of exchanges, the pursuit of oil and money being as strong as the pursuit of gold in Columbus's day. But the pursuit of words? The exchange of ideas? The love and spirit of who we really are, who we intend to be? Those things seem lost. Where did they go? Nowhere, they have simply been cast aside. They still hang over us as angels in the sky.

This collection of *Appraisals* for a poet in India, Kiriti Sengupta, frequently reminds us that we are suffering an odd illness. As founder of Transcendent Zero Press, I believe publication of this collection by an American publisher will bring American readers to a standstill. We tend to think of the United States as somehow different in its problems and contradictions from the rest of the world. Otherness is the shadow of our being projected onto the outsider. Many on the left argue that it is we corrupting the world, while those on the right say we are the Promised Land. Both views neglect the actual truth and hold biases about the mission of this country. The United States is the seat of power and capitalism. Even though we consume much of the world's industry, we must invite the inevitable truth that we are also leaders in democracy. We still chant "Greed is good!" and "The poor be damned!" but these sentiments reflect an overall human darkness. Look on the positive side of this historic coin. We have moved the world and made it richer. In the process, a spiritual tumult has enveloped us and we are at war with all the goodness within us. Is this possibly a sign of our struggle universally? Is there anything eternal in human nature? Does the darkness have light? Why do we waste our lives in decadence? I believe Sengupta's work poses a challenge to our emptiness, and this collection of surveys, reviews, and interviews are a great contribution in this age of post-truth. Post-truth, of course, is political nihilism. Let's learn together that this is something occurring in the world and is not an isolated enigma by any means. Forgetfulness is sometimes arrogant and makes selections through creeds rather than observation. We must face ourselves because it is time. The world must rock like a cradle and the tears must be loosened from our fears. Let's be afraid, but let's seek reminders of beauty, clarity, thought, universality, and commonness. Something in our world wants us to understand.

II.

Let's look beyond the politics for a minute. This book is not political in nature, but I believe it will help heal this country if we heed its essential message. Those who are exposed to the sacred torch presented by Sengupta will not be able to move again without remembering the flame. This healing is only brought by a feeling of deep sacredness, a religion beyond religion's dogmas and creeds. Sengupta was urged toward literature by his wife whom he loves sincerely, and from whom he lives apart so he may continue his craft. She is generous to oblige him. We not only have a mind at work and at play, we have a man with a beautiful romance.

The sacred torch will open your eyes a certain way. In America, Rumi is one of our most beloved poets. Coleman Barks is one of his key translators. The works exceed our own best poets in beauty and knowledge of the divine. Where does this come from? Rumi was touched by the hand of God and led into a fervor of sacred energies. Some things are just destined to happen. Sengupta's journey, entirely without a map for him, may be in God's mind beginning to end. As readers, we are his friends and sympathizers.

This collection will hopefully introduce Kiriti Sengupta to a new audience, stir new hopes and passions in the curious minds of thinking Americans and bring salvation of some kind to the hearts of the hurting ones. It is time we re-assess our values as Americans. Focus on one another and look beyond the heated hatred we have devised against each other. A country remains a country even when it is angry and restless. Please share this book with others. It is not only an author it celebrates, but also a tradition and the hope it brings. We will have to assure ourselves that there is more to life than power, dominance, will, and opposition. There is the love and hope brought to us by God Himself that he wishes we would take advantage of. Kiriti Sengupta, I thank you for enlightening others and for speaking outside our norms, reaching far enough into the splendor of hope for us to realize the imperative of Being.

III.

"Read it in order to get restored within by its healing touch and expression of faith in a value system, pure and simple." This comment from Sunil Sharma on *The Earthen Flute* marks the true importance of Sengupta's work. This isn't something retroactive or a form of limpid fascism that seeks to unify all by wiping out distinctions. Sengupta suffered a major soul search to re-imagine ancient truths and present them in a way that doesn't moralize, condemn, or antagonize the reader. Literature today is angry or nihilistic (depending on the avenue you approach). Everything today in America wants to punch us in the face with our stupidity, violence, and absurdity. We are condemned regardless of what path we take. When Robert Frost wrote "The Road Not Taken", he expressed the regret a choice leaves us. Those options we face but don't move on leave us with uncertainty. What this noble poet does is remind us that optimism can be tragic, and that the tragic element can be healed by the contemplative life.

What is faith in this age? It's a mockery of reason. It's a dismissal of logic and a rejection of ultimate power. Max Planck, the quantum physicist, once remarked that in his studies in physics he was certain there was a divine intelligence behind life. Einstein remarked that science without religion is nothing. I have often said that anything without humanism is moot. Why should I concern myself with anything that doesn't offer humanity a glance at its own grandeur and greatness, or ask it to train itself to enlarge its mind and science? The Renaissance cultivated brilliant minds who reflected this variety of humanism—the depth of it is we have choices: the road to peril or the road to peace. In spite of the increasing pessimism, a look at history should show that we choose peace more heartily. We are a social species and wish the best of others, and often our hearts assume the best of those around us. Sengupta's work is full of instances where that heart beats strongly and actually speaks. "Faith is evidence for things unseen," a quote direct from Scripture, reminds us that we are limited in our perceptions. Perhaps the wasp nest so much of our civilization stirs is empty an only full of phantoms who trick and lie to us.

In exercise, our muscles tear and break. After rest, they rebuild themselves and become stronger and more flexible. An old saying for the post-modern age is, "To create, you must destroy." Writing itself takes a pristine page and spills black ink onto it. However, the page then reflects depth of thought and emotion rather than nothing. The proof of these principles is in life. Human emotions often get the best of us and we fight viciously with our significant others, then we bond again in passionate embraces. Passion is the fruit and fire of life. Sartre wrote, "Man is a useless passion." The burnings and aching of our hearts are seemingly vacuous, but these writings that border on religious remind us that there may be a greater good that will fulfill us. So the vision isn't necessarily religious as much as it is a powerful presentation of virtuous humanism.

Dustin Pickering
May 12th 2017
Founder, Transcendent Zero Press,
Houston, Texas

Preface

Breaking Barriers the Kiriti Sengupta Way

Creative minds are known disruptors. Picasso did that in the year 1937. Joyce, in the year 1921. T.S. Eliot, in the year 1917. Their works disrupted traditional modes of cognition, reception and recording realities in aesthetic terms for a discerning audience open to innovation, freshness and bold experimentation. The avant garde is always challenging — and beautiful! And carries the danger of being incorporated into the mainstream by a swamp called market. Most innovations-turned-cult artifacts have faced such a banality of the literary bazaar of the culture industry. But some survived.

Incorporation vs. Breaking Out.

Often, artists of high caliber defy such reification on the basis of their transcendental vision and freshness that never stales — they can easily afford to be both local and global at the same time. Every age has got such thinkers that redefine boundaries and borders through their experimental works in every field. Artists are no exception to this rule of genius. They are with us and with others of tomorrow. Art has got the strange ability to belong to here-and-now to the tomorrow tentatively glimpsed on the reddening distant horizon. The Bard is both Elizabethan and futuristic in odd simultaneity. Writers! The interrogators. The disruptors breaking down the old narratives and ushering in newer ones of comprehending the universe through various media — collages; murals; pastiches; montage; reportage; nouveau roman; anti-novel; slam; micro poetry and what not.

In India,a similar watershed moment was witnessed in the year 2013. The Kolkata-based Kiriti Sengupta — a successful dental surgeon with tapering fingers and soulful eyes of an artist/singer — whose debut as a poet inaugurated a new kind of writing that balances between belle- letters and profound meditations, in a single breath; the seamless and gentle oscillations — linguistic, emotive, psychological, philosophical, mundane — triggered by a word, memory, event or thing; the young talent coming incognito and then becoming a new sensation in a staid place. In 2013, *The Unheard I* announced the arrival of an impatient writer about to engage work as a demolition-man by breaking stereotypes and sweeping away existing barriers via his multi-layered works hard to classify. The 64-page slim book made Sengupta famous and his mellifluous voice heard across the English-speaking world in few fast months. Since then, his rise has been meteoric; tone critical; gaze restless; style, iconoclastic. Be it wine or earthen flute or water or pen, every element/item/object leads to reflection and perhaps — salvation.

An engaged reader, thinker, critic, Kiriti, like Sartre and Camus, wants to critique the customs, rites and traditions, in a post-enlightenment society. A daring task not performed by many of his well-informed and well-heeled tribe — in this age of post-truth and Brexit. A polyglot and a dentist combine together in a latest avatar and take out the molars that hurt or are decayed in a professional manner and provide relief from pain. His scientific mind questions dogmas; his poetic heart seeks truths eternal, embedded in nature and heritage; a sensitive soul that seeks out novel epistemologies to better understand the complexities of a post-modern, post-industrial, post-rational world where media and other institutions of state and democracy are suspect for being anti-99 percents and manipulate truth and distort news and revamp cleverly — the credibility of a political class bent on closing borders, mental and physical, for power.

Salvation!

Difficult to get in such an apocalyptic world of video games; violence and volatility; hyper-reality; surrealism and a simulated-reality manufactured for a media-obsessed viewers thirsting for more. Salvations are accessible through serious art. Kiriti as an artist attempts such an alternative pathway that provides inner illumination and healing — and subtle transformations by a blend of reflection, poetry, prose and meditation by renewed syntax and words. It is a holistic experience — reading Kiriti.

This collection of high-grade articles on Kiriti Sengupta, the outlier, maps out various contours of his varied, multi-tonal and innovative canvases. Each invited writer interprets Kiriti in a unique manner and appraises his wide universe for his global fans expertly for future research on the maverick. His writings resist nomenclature — like the radicals listed above. They flow with the vastness of the Ganga and contain everything within its broad banks in its long journey to the sea — individuals fusing with the collective; finite with the infinite; guys with the cosmos. The anthology has got critical essays, memoirs and reviews. It hopes to showcase an outsider to the literary world eager for new vices in a mass market. Kiriti Sengupta and his many interpreters lend that freshness only through this singular platform merging all the types of such scholarly venture in a single thread.

He is the new spring!

Sunil Sharma
April, 2017
Kalyan, Mumbai Metro Region,
Maharashtra, India

An Education in Truth through Pursuit

Dustin Pickering

How much do poets and dentists have in common? Well, since poetry is the act of metaphor it can be argued that any profession is akin to poet. In this particular instance, however, I would like to argue that poets are sayers and certainly need clean teeth when speaking lucidly and fluidly. Also, poetry is often like pulling teeth…or *is it*? Does it come fluidly? Does it work its way into your mind and heart with ease? Prosperio Saiz in *The Bird of Nothing* writes, "The rhythmic flow of poetic saying—not the said—pure and simple." This implies that poetry is indeed flowing, something easy and fulfilling. This statement also illuminates the nature of poetics and its relation to poetry. Poetry does not know rules, laws, and concrete guidelines. This is why it adapts to the modern world. Poetics attempts to box poetry in, to define it as a certain thing. Often poets and scholars interpret poetry by describing its qualities and comparing poems. Such work is part of a conversation. However, poetry as its own conversation cannot be crammed into a specific arena. You simply cannot make poetry, a round peg, fit a square hole.

The work of Kiriti Sengupta, a dentist by day, shows the reader how poetry can both define itself and envision whole realities without leaving the world behind. In *The Earthen Flute*, Sengupta's poem "Kajal Deeghi" reads:

"I was inquisitive,

Water here didn't look black,

Nor would I call it green

The lake seemed deep...

Her profound eyes resembled

The nest of a bird

Those eyes,

The water in the lake

They house, and reflect..."

The first statement of the poem indicates a state of mind, a natural curiosity. We are following these impressions in their ambiguity because, naturally, ambiguity leads one to ponder. James Baldwin wrote in "A Talk for Teachers," "Children, not yet aware that is dangerous to look to deeply at anything, look at everything, look at each other, and draw their own conclusions." He further explains that education often leads one to see the society one is educated by critically, to turn on it for its inconsistencies and fabrications. One etymological root of education is "educare." This word signifies a "drawing out." Perhaps what this means is that something deep within, hidden by alternative forces prevailing, is in need of rescuing from the individual mind. This is the sanctity of individual identity, one's right to decide upon matters with personal conscience: the inner logic, brutal and often disconcerting because it even disrupts our own notions of things. Here we are led through Sengupta's own child-like wonderment as he attempts to discern the lake. Does this poem classify as surrealism, impressionism, some modern school of poetry? I honestly have to say no. The way each image twists and turns, perhaps due to its translation, from ambiguity to an unexpected consolidation of objects that have nothing in common superficially, can only be the work of a poet-magician who seeks to grasp the external/objective world by poetic analytical absorption. Sengupta's classical curiosity brings him to ambiguity and finally to poetic revelation.

Note the use of eye imagery. The lake adapts human qualities. The reflections on Kajal Deeghi's waters are not reality itself, but they resemble the truth of a world undefined. Like Narcissus, who is in love with his image in the water, the poet in these lines falls in love with reflection, his own. Everything in this poem is in the realm of seeming. In other words, the reflections are gesturing to another sense. I am reminded of Henry David Thoreau's discussion with his love interest in *The Night Thoreau Spent in Jail*. He asks her to put her hand in the lake, telling her "Being is so much more interesting!" What the lake here houses is "Being."

Is Sengupta more of an observer or an analytical poet? The distinctions are blurred in several of his works. For instance, in "The Encyclopedia" (*My Glass of Wine*, page 26) Sengupta compares the city of Madras to an encyclopedia. "I have not reached yet / the science of you..." This poem reflects an honest humility in seeking understanding. In essence, Sengupta recognizes the depth of the city and the knowledge of it he lacks. Although he knows it exceedingly well, he is not yet *aware*. The prose leading to the poem discusses the city's luminous culture, its diversity of foods and history, and its historic values. Sengupta proudly exclaims his joy at the democratic nature he experiences in Madras. He embraces its traditions, its variety, and the teachings he draws from it. In this chapter of *My Glass of Wine*, Sengupta focuses on the humility his profession expects and the work it requires, but he also reminds us again that appearance is a deceptive thing. To base one's assumptions on a quick glance is foolish. The author's judgments of Madras reveal that he has observed in detail, revealing himself to be a man of the world.

Emerson distinguished between Thinking Man and Man Thinking in his essay "An American Scholar." The difference indicated is between a man who is aware of his place in the world, and one who is flowing with the transitory nature of life. An American Scholar is one who knows and appreciates his specific place in the world. Sengupta writes, "A name is expected to be the gateway of the personality, and individuality." This snippet of wisdom clarifies that identity is something through which we perceive. Again, take a look at the poem "Kajal Deeghi". Perception as a mental phenomenon and an external concrete reality are confounded. We ask, which of the two are dominant? Anthony Storr, British psychoanalyst, writes in *The Dynamics of Creation* that humans are restless animals with huge brains that require continuous stimulation, and our nervous systems are invigorated by this sensual interplay. Storr writes, "The capacity for abstraction gives man a sense of mastery over that from which he is detaching himself." Perhaps Sengupta's analytical approach to Kajal Deeghi serves as mastery over his own curiosity, a curiosity which leads him to self-reflection through the otherness of the world of experience.

My own experiences with Kiriti have varied in nature. We exchange ideas, discuss life and literature, and occasionally bear our souls to one another. Kiriti is a genuine man and harbors certain traits I have found in other authors. In the process of preparing his collection *Reflections on Salvation*, he messaged me to say I had not done enough work on it. He reminded me that he cared for my book, published by his own Chitrangi Publishers. He asked questions that seemed to imply I took too long in doing the work he requested or that I neglected my duty as publisher. I have been in publishing long enough to know that the more serious an author is about a book, the more sharp his or her temper and expectations can rise. I called Kiriti later that evening and let him know I had been at work on the book and had other obligations keeping me busy, but that I cared about the book's production. I poetically added that bringing a book into the world resembles the process of childbirth. The travails experienced by a mother provoke agony and impatience.

Naturally Kiriti was apologetic. When the collection of prose poems came out, the new genre of "flash wisdom," named so by doctorate in linguistics Mary Madec, was born. I was surprised by the book's reception. I understood that Sengupta is magical about attracting and keeping fans who love him for his spiritually practical vision. The book became a bestseller on Amazon within days as a new release in Indian literature, topping several books by renowned authors and translators.

In this fabulous collection, Sengupta writes:

"They say, God dwells within; it is then the mortal exploration of the resort where salvation is largely seen!"

This is the final statement of the collection of "flash wisdom." Jesus Christ is recording in the Gospels as saying that the kingdom of Heaven is within you, and also that his Father's house is many mansions. Keats wrote in one of his letters [To J. H. Reynolds, 3 May 1818] that most people prefer living in the basement to exploring the many rooms of the mind's mansions (Keats refers to "the Infant Chamber" or thoughtless chamber, in comparison to the "Chamber of Maiden-Thought" or the place where sacred thinking begins). Again, Sengupta's profound poetic character aids in is discernment of these truths. The foreword by Casey

Dorman is both critical and eye-opening. Dorman, an atheist, writes, "...Sengupta's message is an expression of the spirituality of faith in the material world." I probably couldn't have expressed my own sentiments concerning the collection better. Salvation, says Sengupta, is not a state for which we strive. Rather, it is a display external to our inner worlds and their dialogues. How often are we led astray today by angry voices or the pledge of self-doubt?

Of course, Sengupta is especially friendly to budding authors. James Baldwin wrote in *Autobiographical Notes*, "Any writer, I suppose, feels that the world into which he was born is nothing less than a conspiracy against the cultivation of his talent." I can testify to this essential truth—myself having been harassed for creating works of art, misunderstood, during times of plight. The encouragement of mature writers who have established their name in literature is something we must not overlook. It seems rare that a poet would reach out to lesser known poets to firmly pull them up the rungs of the ladder. Many writers will advise the public about their craft through books, and speak candidly about their struggles. We do not hear stories of those writers who extend themselves freely to those they admire below them—because, honestly, this is a rare trait today. There are thousands of budding poets looking for publishers and assistance in breaking through. The world today has produced the capacity for anyone to publish a book cheaply or to start an online journal, so the number of poets is soaring. However, the number of success stories are small in comparison.

When we spoke in the beginning of our relationship, I asked a candid question. "Kiriti, are you by any chance a homosexual?" He answered, not in the least offended, "No, Dustin, I am happily married. Why do you ask? Is there something that made you believe so?" When I showed Kiriti an interview between me and my friend Susan Summers for Austin Public Television, he commented that I looked beautiful. I am perfectly comfortable with compliments, but because of my experiences with gay men flirting with me I thought I had put together a serious picture of his intentions. He responded, in kind, that he "took a liking to young authors." That explained it.

The small book *A Freshman's Welcome* serves as proof. The book is an interview with budding young author Tanmoy Bhattacharjee. Mr. Bhattacharjee released a collection entitled *Heights of Life*. In *A Freshman's Welcome*, Sengupta discusses the poetic process with him. Mr. Bhattacharjee states as a final note, "Effort is useless until it forms fruitful action." Bhattacharjee admits that he benefited immensely from the study of English literature, but that literature is more the fruit of one's visions of the world and the personality of the poet. I recall a statement made by a pessimistic poet in defense of his work that poetry emerges from "the personality of the poet." In *A Freshman's Welcome*, the intentions of our noble dentist are again revealed in its epigraph: "Thou shalt love thy neighbor as thyself." The craft of writing is one of the deepest forms of brotherhood, and writers pursue this noblest profession with only small amounts of appreciation.

Sengupta is certainly equipped with the prerequisites to take young poets and writers under his wing. With a bestselling trilogy, a collection of verse that demonstrates outstanding use of metaphor and technique, and the latest bestseller *Reflections on Salvation* which created a new genre, Sengupta has certainly performed well as a poet and writer.

I was puzzled at first when he asked me to write a review for his trilogy. However, I committed to it and saw it published in *Lost Coast Review*. I interpreted his message as sagely religious, questioningly materialistic, and metaphorical. I describe at length the Hindu meditation practice and how it compares to the Biblical symbolism of The Garden of Eden. This interpretation is obviously my own. This reminds us how equivocal and splendid Sengupta's verse and prose is. From it, I was able to delve into deeper metaphors and see similarities between Eastern and Western spiritual traditions. Casey Dorman, editor at *Lost Coast Review*, emailed me with applause. It isn't a coincidence that even he, an atheist, is touched by the thoughts in Sengupta's writings.

The trilogy is united by the common theme of the living experience. *The Earthern Flute*, aptly named, is its own metaphor about folklore and deep earthiness. I connected Sengupta with one of America's most acclaimed poets, Lorna Dee Cervantes, to write a blurb for the book. Cervantes, who is no stranger to these requests, has said she will only blurb a book she absolutely loves. "These poems dwell a language beyond the many borders of languages," wrote Cervantes, a Chicana poet who has read at Library of Congress as one of America's top 100 poets writing today. Imagine if she can enjoy the cosmopolitan nature of Sengupta's poetry, then so too can the readers of this essay!

Reflections on Salvation, published by my own Transcendent Zero Press, is nothing short of groundbreaking work. Any publisher would envy its credit to their list. Although the book appears as a series of prose poems, again appearances are deceiving. The book is a humorous and thoughtful picture of life, of God, and of religious truths and the theology establishment. Kiriti Sengupta, as a true poet and genuine man of spirit, asks that we his readers learn to see and experience things in new ways. He provides signposts. It is our destiny and calling to step beyond, see the open sky, and jump for gladness.

Wordsworth, in his *Preface to Lyrical Ballads*, describes the cultural environment of his world. In 19th Century England, we see in his descriptions a world not unfamiliar. He is irritated by overstimulation through junk journals and trash media, and he seems especially offended by his fellows' consent and contribution to it. This is the world today as much as then. Watch your local news and you hear of violence, warfare, local scandals, irritating discussions of national politics, commercial after commercial designed to exploit your feelings of helplessness and discontent, and of course the inevitable shallow inconsistencies. As an American of the Twenty-First Century witnessing a useless debate between two completely distracted candidates for President, I cannot say these things matter to me any less than they did for Wordsworth.

Wordsworth offers hope for those who see through this madness. He describes poetry as seeking the eternity of the mind, of use of democratic language that speaks directly to the "elementary feelings", and of a celebration of the unique individual. I see something in human nature that distracts itself from its own depths, that turns on its own good will, and uses its own ignorance to dominate others. Perhaps this is where we have all gone immeasurably wrong. Yes, this problem is an immortal malaise.

Nothing true can succumb to this. Sengupta is highly aware of the limited and exclusive rights our frail world permits. The tagline for *The Reverse Tree* states: "trespassers won't be prosecuted…this is all about you & me!" This is another example of Sengupta reminding the reader of his intimacy, of his private thoughts opening between himself and his equal partner the reader. His email signature reads, "My readers are my roses…" In the text of *The Reverse Tree*, we are faced with a sympathetic and honest portrayal of a transgender sex-worker named Lara. His approach to understanding this desolate woman is the same he expects in his readers: an honest openness, slow judgment, and willingness to understand. The human world should be as diverse as the world of flora, and in fact biodiversity is a friend to the survival of species.

His discussions with Lara leave him with his own questions. He wonders why anyone would want to marry a transgender woman who was born a man. This perplexing stranger showed Sengupta the strength in the human spirit. "Living as transgender is not an easy task, to say the least. I have seen Lara managing the role of female that she was not naturally bestowed with, but she was a free spirit who took up the challenge with enthusiasm." [Page 19] This testifies to our author's willingness to step out of his natural human prejudices to see the goodness and strength in a person who represents something profoundly unfamiliar.

In a recent article in *Tuck Magazine*, written by Kaushik Acharya, we are presented with an approach to *The Earthen Flute* as Sanskrit literature. Acharya writes, "Sanskrit literature deals with religious and spiritual subjects and themes. We can analyze the world through visions, one is practical and the other is spiritual." The article further says that Sengupta's poems are relevant to Sanskrit for "spiritual tone and wisdom". A central concern of Kiriti's has been the nature of translation. He discusses this in an article for *Lost Coast Review.* He questions if translation is a major obstacle to getting Bengali poetry into English readership. These problems of translation are frequently discussed among poets. To commit to a proper translation, an understanding of culture is necessary. No translation is exact and may not accurately represent the intended meaning. The bounds provided by each language are strengthened by their unique characteristics. Perhaps Bengali and English poets are too linguistically different to effectively communicate this way. In spite of the considerable cultural differences, with Bengali a deeply mystical language and English more directive driven, commonality can be found. This challenge may reveal questions more intimate to human nature than expected. Translation between cultures is poetic itself because it is analogy—an analogy that compares and contrasts ways of life, manners, and histories. It is an act which makes one mode of thought into another to communicate things which are blurred by the "falling tower of Babel."

At last I come to the powerful review of *Reflections on Salvation* written by Sunil Sharma. In his short commentary he writes, "Through the book of 'random' thoughts, Kiriti undertakes and destabilizes the very act of hermeneutics and sets up the democratic right of the well-informed reader to assert their right and autonomy of their objective reading of a pluralistic text." I believe this summarizes the entire body of work provided by Kiriti Sengupta.

Epitomizing the Free Thinker — Kiriti Sengupta's Democratic Spirit

Casey Dorman

I once told Kiriti Sengupta, in an email, "You epitomize the free thinker who respects tradition—a combination rarely seen." I had just finished reading his book, *Reflections on Salvation*, for which I later wrote a foreword. The small book is a collection of, in the words of Irish poet, Mary Madec, "flash wisdom," a description I find apt for a series of short observations, mostly centering on the topic of renunciation of the world vs. attachment. Without being harsh or insensitive, Sengupta questioned both the value of unattachment as a goal and its practice in those who identify themselves as religious. I imagine that it was a somewhat brave stance in a country where such a concept is hallowed in tradition and in which religious people, such as monks, are probably respected for their lack of worldly attachment. It is not a concept foreign to a Westerner, such as myself, but it is not generally valued in the West, except as an antidote to excesses in valuing material success.

I'm not familiar with Indian literature sufficiently to be able to say how much of what Sengupta writes breaks new ground, but, even with my background of reading experimental and iconoclastic literature from Western writers, I have been impressed with his stylistic freedom and his questioning attitude. The first book of his that I read was *My Glass of Wine*. I was expecting a book of poetry. Instead what I found was a book of personal reflections, written in prose and augmented by short verses. This combination of prose and poetry used to complement each other was something new to me, although Dustin Pickering's review of the book in *Lost Coast Review*, suggested that it might be "a new form of literature being written by Indian writers." Whether or not the style is inventive, I found it refreshing. The poetry expressed an image-laden reflection of what was said more directly in the prose. To those readers who have a short attention span for poetry, in the opening piece in *My Glass of Wine*, the author states that he is hoping to reach a wider audience than typically is attracted to pure poetry. In his words, "I think poetry should not read too abstract! It can be made accessible and enjoyable as well." His book defies classification by genre, a point he appreciates quite well. As he says, "This is a book written in the English-language, and in several ways. Look, by categorizing a book we actually classify the readers." Rather than do this, he invites all readers to join him in the experiences he includes in his writing. This is just one example of Kiriti Sengupta's democratic attitude: he is sharing his experiences and observations with the many, not just the few who consider themselves literary enough to read poetry.

I don't read the Bengali language, so I am thankful that the six books by Kiriti Sengupta that I have read have all been written in English. This is apparently a point of contention among Indian writers and he gives no apology for not writing in Bengali. Sengupta says: "Writing in English is no sin, nor is it a lesser offense. This is just a matter of personal choice." What he does insist on is that he is writing as "an Indian [Bengali] author. I'm a born Bengali and if my writing does not ooze the essence of Bengali culture and traditions, I'm only ignoring my being on the earth." This pushing against boundaries, examining whether they are legitimate or not, is a trait that is illustrated in all of his writing. His religion is obscure to me. He talks of being baptized as a Christian, but also of his Hindu heritage. His description of his Christian baptism as a young adult is ingenuous and a little humorous. In response to drinking red wine as part of a Christian ritual, he reflects upon the role of wine in Hindu Tantric worship. His acceptance of religious meaning and his eagerness for experiencing religious practices appears to be open and eclectic, a rare find in any human.

The Reverse Tree is one of Kiriti Sengupta's most interesting books, at least in my opinion. It is a series of observations revolving around the subject of male identity, or, more broadly, about the many aspects of humanity existing in a single person. The essays and poetry are revealing and are often unflinching in their honesty and their nonjudgmental stance. Particularly, I was impressed by the awareness of and admission of both male and female components in a full personality. In his essay "Crisis" Sengupta describes meeting a transgender person, Lara, who was enduring both a physical and emotional crisis in her life (she was a born-male who was in the process of assuming a female identity). Sengupta's description of his interaction with her is empathic, curious, accepting and contains no hint of censure or judgment. Neither is there any fear of his own sexuality becoming compromised by his interaction. In a word, he sees Lara as a human being going through struggles as any human being does, though the content of the struggles might be different. His poetry acknowledges the male and female sides to a single personality—*"I've my own equation of love/my he throbs in fire/while my she is coy."* In response to questions of the wisdom of writing a poem such as this, he writes, "Ah! I admit that the poem I cited above has a blend of both sexes in a single frame, and although a poem is essentially omni-gender, I won't mind if my readers mark this poem as 'bisexual'." He goes on to cite the presence of a third sex as a category in the Vedic literature. He discusses the presence of laws against homosexuality in India and remarks "I wonder how such a law can possibly exist in the world's largest democracy!"

The Reverse Tree also touches upon racial discrimination, discrimination due to skin color, and attitudinal biases that interfere with moving from one culture to another. One of my favorite of Sengupta's poems is as follows:

they said you were black
they knew they were white
they loved their eyes

the immigration officers were curious

*I pulled my sleeve up to the elbow
showing them the mark
they grinned...*

*and I said
this has been the* Nelson Mandela *patch*

Two of Kiriti Sengupta's books that I have read are all or mostly poetry. These are *Healing Waters Floating Lamps* and *The Earthen Flute*. Despite having been editor of a literary review that published mostly poetry for several years, I am a poor poet and a poor judge of poetry. But Sengupta's poetry is most of all, accessible. It is about the mundane, it is about experience, and it brings the mundane experience in touch with the spiritual and the profound. When I was preparing this essay and thinking about the ways in which Sengupta's writings were democratic, one of my first thoughts was that he focuses upon life's and nature's details, he looks to them for enlightenment and meaning. He does not restrict his attention to "higher thoughts" and he seems to have an absolute faith that the real world about him holds the key to gaining the most from living. He captures this beautifully in his poem, "Experience Personified" from *The Earthen Flute*:

*As I walk along an abandoned playground
In the morning, I see new grasses bathed
In the dew of dawn
Putting off my shoes I stand barefooted
and I walk again*

Tiny droplets envelop my feet
And permeate the skin of my toes

I don't call it a feeling
I would rather name it
My experience

Sengupta's attitude of finding meaning through the ordinary, of gaining profound insights by allowing oneself to be open to all sides of oneself as well as to the myriad aspects of the world around one is not only captured in his poetry, but he expresses it extremely well in a statement in *Reflections on Salvation*, a statement that I described in the Foreword of the book as "refreshing and even astounding." He says "Salvation is but enlightenment, achievable only by actions and through your sensory gateways" —a refreshing thought for an atheist, such as myself, but hardly one to be expected from an Indian poet steeped in the spiritual writings of his own land.

I would be delinquent if I neglected to mention Kiriti Sengupta's generosity, which is both a sign of his personal kindness and also another indication of his democratic attitude. One of his books is *A Freshman's Welcome*, a written version of his speech at the formal launch of the first book of poetry by the young poet, Tanmoy Bhattacharjee. Sengupta's hope, in publishing his remarks, was to "boost the zeal of all struggling poets who wish to become published authors." Apparently the two poets, the older, more experienced one and the neophyte, met on Facebook, another indication of Sengupta's eclectism and democratic attitude in his choice of the media he uses to widen his acquaintances and experiences. In fact, he was attracted to reading Bhattacharjee's poetry partly because the young poet was an academic student of English literature and allied his poetry with a personal "spiritual quest." In Sengupta's words, "My limited understanding of spirituality often leads me to listen to others, especially the new poets who wish to get heard. I was eager to know whether Tanmoy's academic interest and studies have influenced his esthetic and critical consciousness." This is the question of a person who is open to the experiences of others and who is engaged in seeking salvation through his actions and sensory gateways.

Of course one of the most gratifying indications of Kiriti Sengupta's generosity and democratic attitude was his review of my own science fiction novel, *The Peacemaker*, which he generously placed in the *Huffington Post*. He began his review by saying, "I can hear someone is whispering: 'What is Sengupta doing here? Does he not have enough assignments to keep him busy?'" And of course the other question that naturally occurs is *what is an Indian poet doing reviewing an American science fiction novel?* The review was insightful and, being true to the complicated issues of his own spiritual tradition and his naturalistic appreciation of the insights provided by the real world, Sengupta detected an echoing message in my own work. "*The Peacemaker* is an out-and-out spiritual novel that has no strings of religions or prophecies attached to it," he wrote. He had *gotten* the message of my book. I had tried to touch the reader's sense of spirituality through appreciation of the natural wonders around him or her, with no sense of a higher being or force behind it all. And Kiriti Sengupta listened. Now that is an open, inquisitive, accepting and democratic attitude.

Kaleidoscopical Kiln: Kiriti Sengupta's Poems
[from *My Glass of Wine* and *The Reverse Tree*]

Manu S Kurup

'Kaleidoscopical' and 'kiln' are two words that come to my mind when I sit with a Kiriti Sengupta book of poetry. Kaleidoscope is rather too often associated with poetry. But the word 'kiln' got added rather recently as I was sitting with *The Reverse Tree*, in an attempt to solve a puzzle of my own that had been beguiling me for a while. Why was *The Reverse Tree* making itself feel fresh to me every time I pick it up from my library? All the chapters, be it 'Anti-Clock' or 'Crisis' or 'Reversal… Reverse All', make me think for a long time, at times even make me write a few words of my own here and there in the rather unkempt notebook that I carry around as part of my profession as a teacher. Somewhere I read that writing poetry is like making fine pottery; all on skill and knowledge of the craft. If that's true, I thought, Kiriti Sengupta might have a fine kiln at home. That is where the title came from; a small thought originated while basking in an afternoon sun.

In his collection of poems titled *The Reverse Tree*, my favorite book of his, Kiriti Sengupta writes, in a poem inspired by Sumita Nandy's *Desirous Water*.

> *I have matched my lips*
> *with the highs of your water*
> *as you flowed joy*
> *the sun has dared to surface*
> *on your mirror playing both*
> *a she, and a he toy*

As usual when reading a Sengupta poem, the thought takes its own sweet time to strike. When you are a slow reader of books and you have only had a window of fifteen minutes to wake up from the previous poem in the collection in which he wrote,

> *people often accuse me of being poky*
> *I go and meet men with long hair*
> *unhesitatingly…*

> *it was no exception today*
> *I approached him*
> *with a smile on my face*
> *I was about to speak…*
> *he said*
> *I have failed to become a poet*
> *miserably…*

…the apparent conflict of male and female inside a human spirit is what intrigued me and in fact, fueled the rest of the journey. Sexuality, as confusing as it is with all the theoretical debates in academics and media,

Sengupta seeks effortlessly the co-existence of feminine and masculine in human soul. He has his own equation of love. And, it is beyond just 'both the sexes in a single frame.' So, when Kiriti Sengupta makes the third sex, a subject of his poetic imagination titled 'Crisis', providing us with some poems that give deep insight into the matter, it is necessary to acknowledge the intentions of the poet.

my he throbs in fire
while my she is coy

His rather complex relationship with Lara, a transgender sex worker, revealing her inner soul and ambitious plans for life, the tragic setbacks, and the sunny, positive side of living on one's own terms take the reader away from the usual blabber about sexuality to a humane poetic discourse of life. More than these deliberations of souls, as opposed to the usual celebration of souls that we see in the new Indian poetic scene, Kiriti Sengupta's poems make a difference in the way you can see the world. In fact, it can split your perception into 'before' and 'after'. How else can you remember the lines,

Consumed time
like an infant consuming
milk; inevitable
it remains.

Killed essence of
the eternal soul; and consumed,
essentially I remain…

I think the poet must have realized that the poems consume reader more than the reader consumes poems. That understanding is quite evident in the way Sengupta writes. The way the poems 'rain', as the section is aptly titled in *My Glass of Wine*, skipping between love, motherhood and confusion, taking the unready reader through a mountain-pass on a wild whirlwind of poetic memories and experiences, Sengupta is not an easy poet to read. His poems demand a reader with experience of life and its fine nuances. Just like he deliberates on 'reversals' in the end of *The Reverse Tree*, his poems do a reversal on the feelings. In fact, his poetry effectively transcends beyond his many books. For me, the more I read Sengupta, the more connections I find between his many poems though they are all scattered across many wonderful books. Even the seemingly easy, yet philosophically complex interpretation to verses from *The Gita*, reflect the root philosophy of Sengupta poems in a nutshell; the myriad interplays between the shadows of life and its experiences. When he challenges the reader to become a 'bird', the flight scares me but the thought of freedom immediately envelops me in a poetic shell. Thus, the chapters stand tall as if independent from each other. They may be. But what gains importance is the string that connects all these crystal beads in to a fine *mala*. For me, the constant search for the essence of human soul can be seen as an underlying factor in Kiriti Sengupta's poems. He attempts to clarify his thoughts of 'soul' by saying, "*it attracts dust that smears the steps to the body temple.*"

In my first review of Kiriti Sengupta's book *My Glass of Wine*, I wrote that it was beyond any category of books that I had ever seen. It was an earthy amalgamation of thoughts, flowing effortlessly in and out of forms. After reading it twice, I finally reached a conclusion that it resembled that of a painting I had seen in an unknown art gallery in a rather forgotten part of Fort Kochi. It was that of a busy ancient port with different colors. A careful inspection over a few days revealed several other aspects of the painting; the vivid detail of the geography, merchant ships, the fisher folk... but the bleak blue sky that canopied all of this remained the same; a soul crunching feeling of pervasiveness and permanence. *My Glass of Wine* carries that permanence with ease though it tests the reader with a melee of contrasting images and memories. It is not your usual cup of wine because it has a strong philosophical undercurrent that might tug at even the most veteran reader of poetry. As a teacher of mine once said, philosophy freed from religion is easy for soul. Though Sengupta's poems in *My Glass of Wine* have deeply philosophical foundations, it is free of religion in the basic meaning. It shows a deep understanding of a civilization's fundamentals. In that meaning, Sengupta is an essential poet in the times in which civilization as we know it is undergoing a vast, almost uncouth, change.

Kiriti Sengupta's books are kaleidoscopical in nature. Most of these poems, even after given with sufficient context of the poet's own, succeed in forcing the reader to think beyond the poet's intentions and thought-stream. As a wine-maker myself, I understand the varying taste that wine undergoes depending on where you keep it and how often the bottle was used for keeping wine. Human soul, for Sengupta, not only undergoes the same difference of taste but achieves a certain level of perfection if constantly used against the whetstone of poetry. With that as the core philosophy of his poetry, Kiriti Sengupta marks his place among a new age of Indian poetry. His kiln makes fine poetry, instead of the usual pottery associated with the word, and they will stay on in the Indian poetry scene as essential markings of an age in which the collective notion of soul, spirit and spirituality underwent a significant change.

Kiriti*babu*: My experience of a poet as a man

Pranab Ghosh

When did I first meet Kiriti*babu*? Dr. Kiriti Sengupta, the noted poet, who as *The Statesman* headline once declared is no stranger to America. I am not a historian, nor have that bent of mind to remember date and time. Had that not been the case I would have certainly given the exact date and time of our first meeting. But that is not going to take away anything from the poet as a man I came to know later.

It was at the Oxford Bookstore in Calcutta that I first saw Kiriti*babu* as I fondly call him. I had gone there to read my poetry and he too was there to read his. It was an event in the run up to the book fair or more precisely the Kolkata Literature Festival that has become part and parcel of the Kolkata Book Fair for the last three or four years. Kiriti*babu* was seated at the first row and as I completed reading my poem I found him nodding in appreciation. Everyone wants to be appreciated and I instantly liked him. But no exchange of words happened that evening. No one introduced me to him nor did I step up to him to get introduced. We spoke and got introduced the next morning!

Kiriti*babu* was then staying in a rented studio at Sinthimore, a place in north Kolkata. There is a tea stall at Sinthimore that I frequent for the morning cuppa. I had ordered my tea that day and as I looked to my right I saw a somewhat familiar face chatting away over a cup of tea with a young man. With the earthen pot in hand I approached him and as I approached him I recollected. "Did you not read poetry last evening at Oxford?" I asked. That was the beginning. It's close to two years now that I have known the poet, who turned out to be a friend, philosopher and guide to me. To be very honest had Kiriti*babu* not been there I would not have been continuing as a poet, simply because of lack of encouragement.

In three months of my knowing him he became the publisher [who is known to patronize younger talents] of my first book of poems, an anthology that I co-authored with another poet. However, I am not particularly young, in fact I am couple of years older to the poet, but that never deterred Kiriti*babu* from pointing out what he liked and did not like in my poems.

I remember speaking to him one morning over telephone. I mentioned that I have written some four five poems on 'fire'. Pat came his suggestion. Why not write on the five elements a series of 20 – 25 poems and we would have a chapbook at hand. I started dreaming of a book of poems written by me. Had there been no Kiriti*babu* I would not have dreamt and that dream would not have become a reality. Kiriti*babu* can inspire. Kiriti*babu* can guide and finally Kiriti*babu* can deliver. He delivered my book of poems one morning with one sentence, "You will never forget this morning." With the seven author copies in hand I beamed back, "Neither do I want to." Almost one year has passed and my second book of poems is awaiting publication — a Canadian publishing house has accepted my manuscript. I am saying this because without that long morning conversation with Kiriti*babu* where he dwelt on what he would consider good poetry this book would not have been possible. What Kiriti*babu* told that morning changed the way I thought about poetry. I mean *writing* poetry.

I am not going into the details of that conversation. But I will, for the benefit of young readers, give the crux of what he said. "There should be an element of mystery in the poems you write, something intriguing," he had said to open my eyes. Poetry is not a tell-all description of a situation or an emotion but a narration where the untold gathers momentum and charts the path of understanding in a reader. The essence of poetry lies there in the mystery.

Kiriti*babu* is an immaculate editor as well. I came to know this when I translated Bitan Chakraborty's *Santiram-er Cha*. The English rendering is called *Bougainvillea and Other Stories*. Kiriti*babu* took pains to go through each line and compare it with the original. He took particular interest in capturing the true essence of the original. Wherever he found even a minutest discrepancy he wanted me to rework and I didn't mind. At some places he did the changes himself and sought my opinion. His eye for the minutest of detail surprised me!

During the period that I have known Kiriti*babu* three of his poetry books have been published — *The Earthen Flute*, *Reflections on Salvation* and *Dreams of the Sacred and Ephemeral*, a compilation of his trilogy: *My Glass Of Wine*, *The Reverse Tree* and *Healing Water Floating Lamps*. I will not comment on all the books as noted critics have already heaped praise on them. However, I wrote about *Reflections on Salvation* in a piece included in this collection. This book helped me understand the poet as a man better. Kiriti*babu* is not an atheist. He is deeply devout. I experienced this on our trip to Benaras where we went for a book launch. After visiting the Kashi Viswanath Temple we offered our prayers to the Ganges and Kiriti*babu* chanted the hymns as we did. He knows the lines of scriptures by heart. But this does not mean that he is a devotee given to blind faith. Not at all! Reason rules his heart and his faith is purified by his power of reasoning. And this comes out aptly in *Reflections on Salvation* when he writes: "…A renunciate abandons the family — the root and the society, but comes back to them to secure living. Is the monk honest enough to be named a *Sadhu*?" Or "…*The Veda*s did not count on malnutrition; they did not consider environment, let alone poverty." Or "…Divinity might be found in conduct, but not in codes." Kiriti*babu* is against fanaticism and does not believe in religious codification of life. And here he stands out in this age where even our political masters are out to exploit religion for electoral gains.

If rationality forms the backbone of the man as a poet he also excels as a husband and father. For the last five years he has stayed alone — at present he is staying in another rented studio that doubles up as his office — for the sake of his creative endeavors. He wants to devote most of his spare time to writing, and his understanding wife accepts this wish. But this does not mean he neglects his wife or son. He is a loving husband and a doting father who discharges his duties faithfully, however remotely he works. And this speaks volumes of the poet as a man. In the final analysis Kiriti*babu*, as I have known him is a fine poet, excellent editor, encouraging publisher and above all, a nice person who youngsters should emulate.

A Study of *The Earthen Flute* and *Reflections on Salvation*
Dolonchampa Chakraborty

When I get to read a new book of poetry, I give myself a chance to know the poet as well. And the best way that works for me is to select a random page and read the scribbles on it. Ignoring the introduction or the foreword helps me in unveiling the plot which is woven and unwoven through the poems. That experience sometimes equals with that one of an explorer who suddenly discovers a hidden lake in a virgin mountain range, like these lines here at page 25:

> *Wishes are chanted with closed eyes*
> *And we continue to live being frightened*
> ["Gateway to God," *The Earthen Flute*]

The sudden impact of *'wishes'* reminds me that even intimate kisses are also performed with closed eyes, and people who do not close their eyes while kissing their partners are psychologically considered very cold-hearted or insincere. I feel that the emotion these two lines have generated are exactly similar to what I've felt through ages about the religious and ritualistic capitalism that generate fear and thrive on the rules of fear to keep people through generations, irrespective of their religion, caste or creed—blindfolded, cocooned inside their shells of superstitious beliefs; no amount of education has been able to break that shell to enlighten them.

These are rather somewhat accepted norms in today's Indian society and putting these thoughts into a lucid poetic language has not been a consideration in the society of poets - for the fear to be branded as the one who couldn't go beyond the so-called boundary of postmodernism to find words which will seldom make any sense or relate to any depiction of truth.

Astonished at this impact, I take a leap backward and the sketch at page 20 erases the heavy mist from my eyes. Somewhat unmindfully, I look at the poem on its neighboring page and get startled by the name of the poem — "Kajal Deeghi."

The entire title of a poem has been named after a very popular childhood memory—a Bengali rhyme and the visual impact associated to it—so nonchalantly that it almost reduces the memory to a huge nothingness; it rather becomes a reminiscence of youth. Should a poem take that path of telling a story or should it merely be an indifferent narrator of the life it has experienced? In this particular poem, the fear as well as the potency of the color black engulfs the water and it gradually increases to submerge the vision of the reader; it was mentioned, *water here didn't look black*—but that eternal distance between an assumption and the reality is immaculate and the poet never tries to break or cross it. He rather expands its possibilities to that unattainable point where an imaginary woman becomes the love icon of a complete generation.

Is that woman very different from Goddess Durga? Is any woman different than an earthen form of a super-deity for that matter? Our societal practices use the women, worship and abuse them as per necessity, and then throw them out of focus to satisfy the loosely-guarded conformity. Saying this, I wouldn't like to be branded as a feminist which I'm not. I just happen to notice the eyes of a mother which are responsible for a construction, a deconstruction and a destruction of a society and its practices. I wonder, is she herself responsible for this fact also that sculptors forget to concentrate on her third eye—the eye of wisdom and enlightenment? The eyes of a mythical girl—a woman of religious substance become that of an earthly human with one blatant stroke of thought: *It has been kept open/ Full or half* ["Keep An Eye," *The Earthen Flute*]. I realize that the poet has a fetish about eyes—earthly, magical, reluctant, casual, submissive, a certain lifelessness imposed on them.

"Time and Tide" [*The Earthen Flute*] could just be another tale of misfortune. But the improperly done egg-yolks changed the color of the poem to an extremely unwanted white. Had it been a dream, it could be explained as representing an unfortunate woman's unintentional inability to give birth, who at the prime of her youth loses her husband—the gateway to everything formal and established in a patriarchal society. Seeing the stunning use of allegory, I couldn't be sure that it is not one.

A sense of urbanization dwells in the words of the "Cryptic Idiom." At the same time, the poet's profound connection with mythical symbolism is easily comprehended. However, some lines here and there may seem a little too obvious. But, doesn't life itself play the *obvious* many times, making it monotonous and wanting us to break free? It is that urge and courage to deflate, and completely ignore the consequences, and the fear linked to it creates the poet out of a common man who can utter words like a surreal existence:

> *No sorrows anymore, nor a hint of delight*
> *A wonderful world opens up deep inside*
> [*The Earthen Flute*]

Speaking on surreal, poems like "Gateway to God," "Do You Have A Christian Name," and "Struggle for Silence" are as fresh as the first monsoon rain. The poet seems to be in complete harmony with his soul or *self*. This synchronization with one's soul is not easy, and once attained, it keeps one's consciousness tuned to the cosmic rhythm. Hence, what was a mere perception, now becomes an effortless practice.

As I moved to the poet's other book *Reflections on Salvation* [July, 2016], the spontaneity and confidence of my reading of *The Earthen Flute* [January, 2016] was carried forward. By now, I started to feel that God is a concept to the poet of these two books. He is not suffering from any kind of dilemma about his God's gender or prejudice, and therefore, the age-old ritualistic practices are not significant to him—he can easily give humanity a higher place over the much feared and worshipped *'godliness'*.

In a time of utmost restlessness and intolerance throughout the country when murders cannot be attributed separately to political or religious reasons, the book *Reflections on Salvation* starts with the poem, "Saffron." By saying this, I'm in no way trying to prove that this is a poem that stands against or in favor of any particular political opinion. However, some words are opinionated and formed even before they're uttered.

From the very first poem, the poet influences his readers with apt questions or accounts that are generated from the clarity of a logical and literate mind.

"*…with saffron comes sannyas or renunciation, and with renunciation arrives attachment. Attachment with the world, attachment with domesticity, or may be the Gods*".

In present day India, this very word [saffron] has become synonymous with the masking and unmasking of people who have been living together for generations. From that perspective, it is a very bold stance to approach the practice and consequence of spirituality — make observations about it, question it and comment on it with spaces left for other people to join in the conversation.

At the first instance, what might seem a somewhat unmindful observation will stun the reader by posing a question like this: *You perform and we call it a performance. Shakespeare said, "All the world's a stage." What if you have no audience?/ What if you are not applauded?*" ["Stagecraft"]

Will you still act to do justice to whatever role you have in the play? Are you still ready to go on?

Then there are questions asked in these prose-poems which I will not ignore as the inadvertent ones like the one placed in "Cow":

If scriptures are made for the humans, what about humanity?—makes me think—it's reassuring to find out that someone still cares! It's a refreshing change!

The prose-poetry in *Reflections and Salvation* follows the process of detoxification and purgation of the long-stored and forgotten waste materials which have started to take a toll on the society. A poet may not choose to lead or be a part of a procession with placards and fists, but his words create equal and more forceful impact and it is absolutely a poet's responsibility to be a part of the life—its negativity and positivity that surround him. "Paradise" is one such piece that presents a very mundane and middle-class scenario and then poses a question at the end—bringing the mirror to the readers if they're still hesitant about facing it: shouldn't the woman who sacrifices her whole life for her family get a preference from her family in return during her lifetime only and experience the heaven on earth?

"Krishna" and "Instinct" are profoundly and directly atheist in their treatment. One thing that I find very unambiguous is that, this book very boldly points out the lack of spirituality and its understanding in our daily practices of religion and scriptures. Being religious and being spiritual are two totally different aspect of the same thing… a man can be deeply spiritual thinking that he's extremely religious, while an atheist can be a very spiritual person in his living and thinking. It seems to me that it is an unfathomable space which this book deals with perfect freedom of speech. This book also satires the much coveted atheism in present generation, which is an expression of nullifying the concept of God, as practiced in Hinduism. The basic and advanced Vedic knowledge and its explanation, practices, its history and roots are nowhere related to that trendy part of the fashionable atheism.

Humor, satire, and sensitivity have all been taken into consideration while penning these two books, and the first two qualities have etched their impact on the sharp edge of the messages, without failing to hit at the right place at the right time, delivering the intended impact.

Kiriti Sengupta Makes His Way to Sanskrit Literature through Indian English Poetry

Kaushik Acharya

There are plenty of Sanskrit texts like *Pancatantra*, *Hitopodesa*, *Abhijnanasakuntalam*, etc., and even *The Ramayana*, *The Mahabhartata*, two immensely popular Indian epics, which have been successfully translated into several other languages down the ages. If we observe carefully we can understand that there are hardly any Indian or foreign literature that has been translated into the Sanskrit language. Does Sanskrit literature refuse to receive inputs from texts written in other languages? We have no viable answer here. We probably have never considered or tried to include them in Sanskrit literature as we think Sanskrit bears traditional glory, and an attempt to include foreign texts will only weigh it down and above all, we don't just need to include those texts into Sanskrit literature. People often question the flexibility of Sanskrit language. A language or literature can exist freely if it is flexible, welcoming and accepts wisdom from external sources. Sanskrit literature, perhaps, lacks in these attributes.

It is high time we accentuate the treasures of Sanskrit literature. Students who are studying the subject should necessarily be aware of contemporary world literature. Of late I have translated a few poems by well-known Indian English poet, Kiriti Sengupta, and I have rendered them into Sanskrit owing to their spiritual connotations. Let me cite both the original and translated versions here and my thoughts on them.

sampasya

*trisu netresu durgayah trtiyam tu
adyaiva aparivartaniyam asti,
ayam tu ardha unmuktam unmuktam va
loke avalokyate*

*visaye' smin vigrahakara api udasinah santi,
pasya—
te parthivanetrayoh vivartanam krtavantah yuge yuge,
na tu trtiyam*

Keep an Eye

Among those three eyes of Durga
The third one has been the same
Over the ages

It has been kept open
Full or half

Sculptors never bothered

They have been experimental
Only on her earthly eyes

[*The Earthen Flute*, page 15]

Sanskrit literature basically deals with religious and spiritual subjects and themes. We can analyze the world through visions, one is practical and the other is spiritual. The saints usually describe the reality of life through their spiritual vision, which is impossible through the earthen eyes, but the third eye, otherwise known as the inner eye, plays a pivotal role in envisioning the self.

In some traditions such as Hinduism, the third eye is believed to be located around the middle of the forehead, slightly above the junction of the eyebrows. In this poem, "Keep an Eye," we become aware of the fact that the third eye has remained the same down the ages, like the third eye of Hindu goddess Durga. Even the artists and sculptors have tried their hands in other aspects of the deity, like dress, color, etc. except the third eye that represents spiritual vision or a symbol of self-realization.

I think the poem is extremely relevant in Sanskrit literature not only for its translation-value, but mostly for its spiritual tone and wisdom, which are integral of the said literature.

jatharah

pratikampanam prthivyah anubhuyate maya,
mataram prati aham samyak-prayatnaya
asamarthah abhavam

punah mam jatharastham
kartum tasyah svadhikarm vartate

janami adhunapi,
sa prabhuta-yatnasila bhavisyati
yatha sa purvam eva krtavati

bho jagata! yady-api parthiva-lopaya
bhavantah alocitovantah bhavanti,
mata hi kevalam prasavapidavagantum saknoti

Womb

With every earthquake I realize
I have failed to express
Much attention
To my Mother

She has a right to take me into her
Again

I know she will take
Enough care
As she took before

World, you may comment on material loss
Only the Mother understands her rupture pain

[*The Earthen Flute*, page 17]

We are attached to our mothers who often become a subject of description in literary works and Sanskrit literature is no exception. Mothers are not only the ones who give birth, they can raise children to be called a mother. Poets and philosophers frequently consider the earth a mother. In *"Bhumi Suktam"* of *Atharvaveda* we find the earth as goddess.

mata bhumih putro aham prthivyah [*Atharvaveda* 12.1.12]
[*The earth is my mother and I am her son*]

Since Vedic period the earth has been worshipped in connection with its various utilities in life. Mother earth takes care of us in many ways; we are born and brought up on the planet, we live, and finally, we die here in the earth.

In this poem, "Womb," we can realize our responsibility to Mother earth. But, humans turn selfish as they fail to acknowledge the contributions of Mother earth to their lives and with modernization of human race they tell upon her with every passing day. Even the mother has a right to revolt from being suffered by the indifference of her children who receive much nourishment in the womb for months. In this poem we understand the reality of extreme deception that affects Mother earth which the sages upheld in Vedic hymns and prayers.

vedhasah toranmargam

prarthanasu pranah santi,
ta anirvacaniy anubhutih

tasu asmakam tarsah lavate
suraksitam asrayasthalam

evam parthivanandaya samrddhilavaya ca

vayam prayah bhitasantrastah bhavamah

asa hi mantrita bhavanti nimilitakse,
vayam ca bhitacakitah san jivanadharanam kurmah

anivarya-mrtyuvat ko'pi virat devah
samyak avirbhutah bhavati

Gateway to God

Prayers carry lives within
They are expressions
Our desires take refuge in—

For all worldly pleasures and fulfilment
We remain scared, perhaps

Wishes are chanted with closed eyes
And we continue to live being frightened

Like an inevitable death
An enormous God steps in

[*The Earthen Flute*, page 25]

The Vedas are the first texts in the library of mankind. In them we could find the tradition of holy *mantra*s which were chanted to please the gods and goddesses. The concept of God came from the destructive patterns of Nature, and from a strong belief of her supernatural prowess like fire, storm and thunder, drought and flood, etc. In *Rigveda* the sages practiced Vedic hymns for a better life and afterlife.

In this poem, "Gateway to God," we find a characteristic human behavior during prayers. We keep our eyes closed being frightened of both God and death. Death is not necessarily a loss of life, it can be described as an abolition of dreams and desires. During Vedic times the sages used to reflect on their inner realizations and renounce worldly pleasures to achieve God. They were barely afraid of anything under the sun, except for their fear of being detached to their spiritual practice. Austere practice opened up their inner eyes that envisioned the futility of earthly fulfillments. "Gateway to God" is an original masterpiece of world literature and Sanskrit literature as well.

[a]kalamanudanam

*gurubharikah kaksapavanah
pita putram ahuya asandam asou
datum aicchat*

*mata uvaca: "siddhantam idanim asamicinam adhuna,
sighram idanim gurubharam putraya,
yaccha mama putram plabitum."*

*pita na jnapitavan adyapi paricare, yat—
ayacanam tasya abhyanujnatah adhipurusena,
sa ca avakasaya anumanyate.*

[Un]Timely Grant

The air smells heavy
Father calls up his son
He wants to offer him
The chair

Mom says, "It is too early for him,
Let my son keep afloat!"

Father is yet to inform family,
Boss has approved his prayer
and he is allowed to leave.

[*The Earthen Flute*, page 57]

Since time immemorial a father plays the main role in his family. He acts as the chief; the role of a leader. The growth and prosperity of a family depends on its leader. In ancient India a father often ruled the family from being the sole provider. In this poem, "[Un]Timely Grant," we realize the importance of the provider in a family. The following Sanskrit verse depicts the essential qualities and duties of an ideal father:

*annadata bhayatrata, vidyadata tathaiva ca
janita copaneta ca, pancaite pitarah smrtah*

[*Chanakya Niti*]

Who could be considered a father? The one who feeds you or provides food, one who keeps you away from fear, one who educates, one who caused the birth (biological), one who performs the sacred thread ceremony. These attributes qualify one to be called a "father." The most famous verse comes from *The Mahabharata:*

pita svargah pita dharmah pita hi paramam tapah
pitari pritimapanne priyante sarvah devata

[My father is my heaven, my father is my religion, and he is the ultimate penance of my life. If he is happy, all gods are pleased.]

In "[Un]Timely Grant" we can figure out a father of contemporary era. But the basic pattern is the same as before. A father works until he retires, but he continues to dominate the family. As he approaches retirement, the father offers the chair (position) to his son, but a mother rarely considers her son grown up and declines her husband's proposal. In reality we love to be governed by our fathers or father-figures and this stunning, short verse succeeds to grab the attention of the readers.

samaya sramam

kascid prstah kimaham
vidyamanam abhasanam abhijanami...

atha anubhabami,
katham tu manusya anubhavanti samah?
iyamavastha kim purnah ravabhavah?
kim rabakarah daivayogad api samam ahvayati?

sangharsinah bhavamah vayam ekavastha praptaye,
yatra iyam murali kadapi na sabdayate-
tatra vayam svasarahita'pi samitah bhavamah

*aikantika-samvaditah bhavisyamah ca vayam
visvakarakamadhye*

api ca parthivamilanavasane nrpocita niravata virajate

Struggle for Silence

Someone inquired if I was aware of existential silence...

But then, how do people perceive quietude?
Is it a state of complete absence of noise?
Does clamor invite peace, by any chance?

We are, perhaps, struggling to achieve a stage
Where the flute won't sound anymore;
We will remain breathless, but relaxed
And in complete harmony with the creator!

Quiet grandeur prevails over
The pinnacle of worldly communion

[*The Earthen Flute*, page 59]

Life and afterlife have secured a major part in Vedic philosophies. In *The Vedas*, there were three stages of life: student-ship, household-ship and retirement. During *Upanishadic* era, Hinduism expanded to include a fourth stage of life: complete abandonment. In Indian philosophy, silence, which has a vibration of its own, refers to peace of mind, inner quietude, *Samadhi* and absolute reality. The ancient texts insist upon proper understanding of silence by experiencing it through complete control of breath and tongue that leads us to a state of eternal bliss. People may refer it to as "death," but we all are approaching to this ultimate stage through the journey of life.

This poem, "Struggle for Silence," bears a deep spiritual undercurrent. Here Sengupta questions if anyone is aware of the ways to achieve inner peace that we long for. But then, he answers on his own. Sengupta emphasizes on being "breathless, but relaxed," a state that is achieved only by the yogis. Yoga, as *The Gita* suggests, refers to the actions that enable one to unite with the Supreme Being, otherwise known as God.

We can relate this poem with the Vedic and *Upanishadic* thoughts about ultimate silence: "*Samadhi*," or "death." We are headed towards the former through yogic practice or towards the latter through our usual course of life. Death is always the ultimate, worldly reality of life and it is evident in philosophy as well as in literature. This poem makes a special place in the sea of wisdom and claims to be included in Sanskrit literature by its inherent merit.

Reference:
Sengupta, Kiriti: *The Earthen Flute*, Hawakaal Publishers [Calcutta]; First edition, February 2016, ISBN-13: 978-93-85783-58-6

How to Use Poetry to Drive Home the Point
Casey Dorman

I read Kiriti Sengupta's trilogy *My Glass of Wine, The Reverse Tree* and *Healing Waters Floating Lamps* in the order in which I think they were written and the order in which I have listed them. To read them in sequence is a journey, whether your own or the author's may be inconsequential. The journey is one that draws the reader further and further into personal reflection—but reflection from the world around us into the inner self. Worldly observations become the occasion for explorations of meanings: of the self and its status within the world and within consciousness, and of life's journey from birth to death.

Both *My Glass of Wine* and *The Reverse Tree* contain more prose than poetry. The first volume is almost innocently self exploratory and revelatory: the poet's first encounter with literature [in the context of his first date with his future wife], his family, his sister, his son, his city of origin. He explores his own religion and is introduced to Christianity, an introduction, which he, as a young man, attempts to make the most of, but disappointingly so. Each topic provokes a poem to capture its essence. We see not only the relationship of poetry to that which is meaningful in the poet's life, but the evolution of his ability to express these meanings in poetic lines. *The Reverse Tree* explores even deeper roots of personality and experience. Momentary but memorable encounters with friends [as in "In Others' Shoes"] teach the poet a lesson, which he generalizes to become a lesson for all of us about life. In "Long… a Metaphor" he explores the role of long hair in the poet's definition of his identity… and touches upon the multiple sexual identities that inhabit each of us and become the core of his long essay "Crisis." This beautiful uninhibited exploration of sexual orientation and its relationship to one's humanity moves from an examination of the poet Sumita Nandy and her work, to India's bias and discrimination against homosexuality to a personal narrative of an encounter with someone who is transgender. This latter episode is a model of valuing the worth of the individual and not being distracted by his or her sexual orientation, despite that being such a large factor in the person's identity.

Finally, in *Healing Waters Floating Lamps* the author becomes a full-fledged poet, abandoning, for this volume, the use of prose to express his meanings and relying completely on poetry. The results are stunningly beautiful. The themes that were initiated in the earlier works are here [as are some of the poems], as is Sengupta's close observations of the world around him. Again, we see the power of the real world to provoke the deepest of inner meditations. The first four poems all focus upon water: the river Ganges and its power to cleanse the soul and tears flowing from the eyes in rivers, being reminded that "Not all rivers succeed to unite." Stone statues and their making provide a window into the spirit. And my favorite, about the yearning [and futility] of becoming more [or different] than you are, and the sense of humor to accept it, is a poem titled "In Dusty Feet."

I was about to prostrate,
But refrained from paying an obeisance
To the enlightened Master
His great toes housed
Some holy grains of dust
He too good care of his feet, I guessed,
And I picked the grains as quickly
As to place them on my head

I followed his footsteps,
Even on the dusty roads
I wished to become such pious grains
So as to stay attached with his feet forever

I turned back as I failed,
And could not hold the grains either
On my big toes…

God remained thumb-sized with dusty feet.

While Sengupta's poems touch the spirit, and often deal with spiritual matters, they are uniformly grounded in the world around us. No better example is his poem, "Scratches are Only Human" and its memorable lines:

> *Few beautiful scratches, deep within,*
> *Soft marks, palpable even after months—*
> *No wounds, but tiny scratches brown*
> *Soothing, mesmerizing in between*

Kiriti Sengupta's three books are not just a journey, but a commentary on how to use poetry to express that which is inexpressible otherwise, even in prose. They accomplish this task very well.

Waiting in the Garden of Eden
Dustin Pickering

I read Kiriti Sengupta's three collections *My Glass of Wine, The Reverse Tree,* and *Healing Waters Floating Lamps.*

My Glass of Wine advocates a return to religious principles and compassion. The author truly believes the world left a sane compassion and sweetness when it began to deny the truths of religion. Sengupta discusses everything from namesake to the Bhagavad Gita in this prose and poetry collection. Lately I have noticed a new form of literature being written by Indian writers. A combination of prose and poetry that mutually complement one another is emerging from this sacred land where literature is honored and adored. *My Glass of Wine* fits this category and is a national bestseller. We are first introduced to Sengupta's key concepts in this small volume.

His work reads like an exploration of life — seen from the Yogi's angle — and an acceptance of its universality and uniqueness. We are taught that Yogis meditate to bring the Mother to the Father, a metaphorical journey that describes the climb of energy up the spine in meditation. Much of Sengupta's imagery stems from this symbolic process.

There is one odd poem in *Healing Waters Floating Lamps* called "Fish-Lip" that seems to have caught the Foreword writer's attention as well. It turns from the imaginative and accessible to the strange and uniquely personal symbolism presented by the author. In this poem, I am reminded to review the opening thoughts of the book:

On the ascending shoots
Your fear matures
A few apprehensions as well
Your roots hold it tighter
Desperately deeper

And much deeper rests your God

This reminds me of the poetry of *The Reverse Tree*. I am also brought to the Biblical proverb, "The fear of the Lord is the beginning of wisdom." Wisdom is distinctly universal and perennial in its goodness. Much life is lived before it presents itself and is brought to the light. Fear is what brings us closer to our deepest values; we feel the world tugging at our Selfhood, wanting to avenge its confusion; and, we cling tighter to our sense of Self as our roots are exposed upward. *The Reverse Tree* is an extended metaphor for human nature, a life of service, and just how strong we as people must become to expose our graces toward others. "With service evolves dependence, and honestly, it is the ladies who turn out to provide better shade than the men," Sengupta opens in the first chapter. Why then is the tree commonly conformed to men? Being flows through all things like water and wisdom is the greatest joy. Sengupta quotes the Bengali of Tagore, "I envisioned the external through the light of my eyes." The Soul is God Himself, so the light of the eyes is the revelation we experience as we live. The Soul is Master, Commander, and the lens through which we perceive our golden glories.

I think a bit on the Garden of Eden and the allegory it presents in light of this book. Much of the myth's imagery can be reconciled with the Guru's meditation metaphors. Adam and Eve as Father and Mother, but the Mother turns away instead of rising up toward the Father. She is "tempted", perhaps distracted, by a wise and clever serpent. This serpent is assumed to be the Devil in traditional interpretations. Perhaps the snake is rather a symbol of the spine, and this allegory reflects the very same wisdom as holy India's religion! The Mother turns directly to the spine, and takes its advice to eat the fruit [the core of the head where the Father and Mother meet], and the result is the expulsion of the couple—yet they are expelled as one, in unity. The snake is forced to consume dust—recall the dust that accumulates on our self-image. Adam and Eve have already attained wisdom but are now guarded from picking the fruit of the Tree of Life. This Tree is protected by a young angel with a flaming sword. This is symbolic of the process mentioned in *The Reverse Tree*:

"Removing agony from life is not an easy task unless we recognize the source. This is all about the worldly attachments that we grow knowingly or unknowingly..." Even the great Sufi poet Rumi explores the tarnishing of Self by worldly attachment. Our humanness is distinct in worldly attachments. They are why we live.

Why does Eve turn from Adam after all? In Genesis 2:7, there is a pun on the Hebrew "Adam" and "adama" — adama means "ground". It is woman, Eve, a reflection of Man, who turns him from the Garden and worldly pursuits to knowledge of good and bad. Adam is a reflection of God in his dominion over the fertile plain, yet he is evicted from his paradise and punished with death. To know good and evil is a death itself, the "sickness unto death", the separation of Self and Other, and the hesitation we experience in our apprehensions. God, wise and primal, tricked the original couple by putting the pieces in place — expecting them to learn the powerful lesson they would only understand from experience. A very similar expulsion and detachment occurs during Adam's sleep when Eve is brought from his rib. We are taunted with reminders of our origins we cannot understand. Things aren't ideal for this very reason. We learn distinctions. We learn judgment, the very vice the Savior advised us to harness. The cherubim and its revolving sword of flame, mentioned in Genesis 3:24, are acknowledgements for the insatiable quest of humankind to find permanence and its ultimate truth of origins.

Sengupta, page 36 of *The Reverse Tree*:

"and the wounds surface again
in all directions...
sporting the guise of **youth**..."

Is he not reflecting the same paradox?

Eve, mother of all living, is cause of our mysterious life and our long thirst for paradise. She was the first to survey the land and truly seek dominion in ways her husband could not imagine. She implores him to remember her birth so he can find himself. *She* was the one in true service to the betterment of humankind by fulfilling human destiny, and leaving a legacy of wonders.

Dreams of the Sacred and Ephemeral
— a review
Duane Vorhees

In the "*Alap*" to his trilogy *Dreams of the Sacred and Ephemeral* [2017] Kiriti Sengupta makes an important point: "Poetry deserves to have more than one layer of meaning. If we remove metaphors, poetry loses its charm. If we remove the philosophical content, poetry turns disastrously mundane." The book, a collection of his earlier volumes, *My Glass of Wine* [2013], *The Reverse Tree* [2014], and *Healing Waters Floating Lamps* [2015], is a rambling yet disciplined journey through the Bengali alleyways of his life. The short prefatory verse "*It was not only the wine, but / that the glass was mine*" well expresses much of its spirit [both in the philosophical and imbibing sense]. Though the themes are varied, it is the "wine," his religious exploration that most closely ties the book together as a genuine trilogy rather than just a collection of verse.

The first book begins with a confession of his ignorance about literature until challenged by his future wife on their first date. From that embarrassment, and his frantic effort to overcome a poor first impression, he emerged as a poet, someone able to realize and express the essence of poetry: *"in all works imperishable I listen to the / unheard... bundles of joy, drops of eyes / make the 'I' a bard."* Immediately afterward, in the second chapter, the book moves to the confession of his early erstwhile conversion to Christianity. Two things stand out to him: the way the congregation was able to unite in prayer "towards the fulfillment of a certain goal" and his first alcoholic drink, homemade communion wine. He was told that red wine made him remember "the divine blood that Jesus sacrificed!" but he remained skeptical of the claim. He went on to discuss similar *Tantric* and *Qurbani* rituals and concluded that "the elements of blood, power, alcohol, and red [are] associated intimately with divinity." In "The Scripture" he realized that *"God only dwells / within mortal frame!"* but it took him some time to discover his personal attachment to *Kriyayoga*. One of its attractions was that there was no requirement to remember God by drinking wine. Instead, the aspirant is able to taste "the rich nectar wine" secreted from the cerebral region; *Kriyayoga* "allows one to reach beyond the mind," and, once spiritual awakening is achieved, it allows one to feel like living in a "winy trance."

I have not reached yet
the science of you

Since period unknown
you spin, and continue to swivel;
you have a firm grip.

Faulty are my limbs,
they tilt even on the steady floor;
I readily realize
it is all in my mind
as the sky swings.

You spin, and continue to swivel.

Much of the remaining text, over the span of all three volumes, can be read with this orientation in mind. The first two contain far more prose than poetry, but the third is all verse. Perhaps it took him that long to find his firm poetic footing. Though not haiku in form, they are, in effect: koan-like enigmas that reveal little while exposing everything. Dr. Sengupta [a dental surgeon] offers healing via a process of self-revelation rather than didactic preaching. They are fine examples of an erotic ecstasy that is simultaneously sensual and spiritual.

The rainbow has disappeared a long time ago
The horizon looks clean and sunny
as the rain dropped in seven hues

In those drops of color I remained
I remain even now
I...
And you were the drop-filled windy cloud

Who is being addressed? Is it a love poem or a benediction? One's answer colors the perception. As he admits, "It keeps the human alive in my wine!"

A translator of the *Bhagavad Gita*, he reminds us of a passage about "an imperishable banyan tree that has its roots upward and its branches down and whose leaves are the Vedic hymns. One who knows this tree is the knower of The Vedas." To Sengupta, this is key: "Humans are the only such trees that have their roots [brain] up and the branches [limbs] down." He ruminates on this insight by offering up a number of arboreal poems.

My tree is stout, / well-developed / it refutes the gravitational pull // not always, you know… // my roots run against the sap!

In "Wide," one of the poems from the first book, he insists, "*Your roots hold it tighter… desperately / deeper / and much deeper rests your God…*"

Elsewhere he claims "*numerous branches of the root / unite into two soft halves*" … "*nature shelters the root / secures within an encapsulating tough skin // the shoot is long and thick / smoother skin palpitating beneath. / no study of the plants, but of humans*"

The final volume is infused with the mystic nature of the Ganges. It opens with "Beyond The Eyes": *I reach the sky / While I draw a circle in the water // Looking at the image // I take a dip*

In the same poem in which he recognizes that the "unheard … bundles of joy" made him a bard, he admits:

defining soul is difficult,
rather impossible
I have no doubt
I can perceive the 'I' in every decibel

my take is simple
it attracts dust
that smears the steps to the body's temple
I press two fingers firm on my ears, and thus,
let the light dazzle my imprisoned candle

I walk early morning, wrapped in fresh silk
air entices, my skin shivers – I hear sounds
of click

He, thus, sums up how his poetic existence is connected to, and dependent upon, his spiritual; and under the Gangetic influence his verse progress from the naturistic to the mystic: "*Immersion happens only in the water / People gather…they sing and dance / Only a few of them have their eyes moistened // Rituals of self-reflection end / With gods and goddesses / The river turns pregnant*"

Until finally, in a wryly ironic "Memorandum of Understanding," he is able suggestively to join the poetic with the spiritual and biographic elements of the trilogy: "*I'm no linguist... // I know / air and age are linked... // and the wounds surface again / in all directions... / sporting the guise of youth...*"

As an American reader, I would have appreciated more contexts [although I'm sure Indian readers and foreigners who are familiar with Indian culture would have found such commentary tedious and unnecessary; it's always problematic how one deals with separate, disparate audiences]. Nonetheless, I found the parts of the book that did try to provide explanation — the long personal essays that comprised most of volumes one and two — far less compelling than the elusive poetry that did not try to "explain" anything. These poems are simultaneously specific to Sengupta and universal for any reader with the patience to see them not as "the answer" to life's mysteries but as a clue to one of the possible answers. Any enlightenment from the poem derives from within the reader as much as it does from the poet himself. There is such a thing as good didactic poetry, and poets who are supremely able at directing others' attitudes and behaviors. These poets act in the twin roles of hold keeps and locksmiths. But there is also good poetry that suggests infinitude of doorways and displays panoply of keys while omitting the labels to match any key to the correct lock. The creators of these poems are enablers who encourage others to, first, pick the doors and, second, to try to pick the locks. The tools are provided but the instructions are unclear, written in a familiar language undefined in the standard dictionary. It is to the second category of poets that Sengupta belongs. His poems need no cultural context [beyond knowing what a tree is or water or self, those things which are innate and self-evident to nearly everyone]; they "merely" require enough insight or imagination to allow their reader to understand, for instance, how a mother bird can change into the sky [as he suggests in one of his masterful verses].

Thoughts on Reading *The Earthen Flute* and *Reflections On Salvation*
Duane Vorhees

A lot matters
if you remember
the name

Most commentators on the poetry of Kiriti Sengupta rightfully concentrate on his earthy spirituality. But they often fail to recognize that this quality is firmly rooted in his sense of selfness.

"Let us be name-filled," as he exhorted in an earlier volume, *My Glass of Wine*. He noted that "names bear meanings, and have their own charm that we generally associate with the persons concerned," adding that Rabindranath Tagore had suggested that a name assists in the beautification of people via imagination, since their beauty can't be entirely comprehended through our senses. So, according to Kiriti, "A name is expected to be the gateway of the personality, and individuality."

After pointing out that many Indians are named after deities, "thankfully" he was named after "an important character of *The Mahabharata*. And he was no god." However, he modestly failed to note that "Kiriti" was actually one of a dozen alternative names for the epic's central character, Arjuna [because he wore the celestial diadem of that name, which had been presented to him by Indra, the ruler of the gods]. Arjuna's tutor Drona [an incarnation of Brahma himself] realized that, of all his pupils, Arjuna was the only one with enough focus to shoot the eye of a bird in a tree. As a poet, the metaphorical ability to do so distinguishes Kiriti in his best work.

Often his preoccupation with his selfhood is muted, but it is seldom absent [though, indeed, it is frequently self-effacing in a humorous, ironic manner]. He professes to be puzzled by that fact that his older sister has always called him "Bhaiya" [which means older brother in Hindi], and much of his spiritual quest seems to be engaged in a search for his true identity. He regards himself as both a Christian and a Guru-directed practitioner of Kriyayoga, and in "Do You Have A Christian Name?," one of the poems in *The Earthen Flute*, he remarks that "*People tend to ask me hesitantly / if I have a Christian name.*" His reply, however, has evolved; he used to answer that "*A name is usually pre or post-natal*" but now he says, "*I'm not sure if Jesus offered names.*"

He entitles one of his prose poems in that book, "Clues to Name." The poem is a meandering, elusive, elliptical search for a personal mantra [etymologically, "instrument of thought"], variously described as a sacred utterance, a prayer, a spell, a numinous sound [analogous to birdsong] that may or may not have syntactic structure or literal meaning though, typically, melodic and mathematically structured in a way that is resonant with some spiritual quality such as truth, reality, light, immortality, peace, love, knowledge, action, etc. Like bird song, mantras have the ability to communicate. In Tantric tradition, mantras are deeply personal rituals, based on codified esoteric traditions, passed on from a Guru to a disciple through a prescribed initiation; in this school of religious thought, each mantra is a deity. Kiriti's poem [partially abbreviated here, though some of the ellipses are part of the original] is similarly phonetic and syntactic, but not semantic: "*An experiment I undertook. A seed slept in dark, clueless; no viable chant ... A tree stands with its green veil. Through its branches I noticed the ascent of sap, but it had no salt. Some names sweet ... some seeds added at source! As one finds it apt! Just the way the mind seeks. My mind. Mantra bears lust ... petty you, you blame the luster! Lust reinstated ... inevitable it is ... Immersion via the mirror ... goodbye to the goddess, but the lion keeps awake with his eyes closed ... Fists full of water and free donation ... serving the pilgrims ... Your wisdom runs into the lustrous hole. Incenses are not burnt by wet hands, they say. Prohibited it is. Water has no call, no decor either; it floats the bone and the mortal frames free!*"

In a more conventional verse he bemoans,

Much hassles to envision the self—
A mirror fractures to kill the dreams...
And I patiently await
Unveiling...

In the volume *Reflections on Salvation*, Kiriti returns to this central refrain again and again:

"What if you are not applauded? You might blame your luck, but did you deliver your best? Salvation is but enlightenment, achievable only by actions, and through your sensory gateways."

"I would rather worship myself and be happy. My physical frame, words I utter, and my mind — they have one thing in common: 'I.'"

As he consistently and repeatedly confesses, in tome after tome and poem after poem, for Kiriti, the process of absorption into divine selflessness is inextricably connected to his own assertion of self.

Sacred and Ephemeral — "*Vision or a waking dream?*"

Tuhin Sanyal

It is really immemorial since when critics of poetry came to be loosely considered as clinical people, who actually dissect poetry and try to wittingly pry into the poetic psyche, or into the poet's persona. We cannot always blame the Freudian schools for such modernistic levity, nor can we fully agree with Derrida's observation "*Il n'y a rien en dehors du texte,*" in a deconstructionist's manner, irrespective of whether it means "*There is no outside-text,*" or, is mistranslated as: "*There is nothing outside the text.*" Thankfully, myself a poet, though doubling up as a critic of Kiriti Sengupta's 'Trilogy' at the moment, I do honestly believe that all texts have an "Ephemeral" beyond [or 'outside' to] themselves. And for such belief we do not require authorial permission, nor theoretical scaffolds for piling up criticisms with ease. Kiriti Sengupta's *Dreams of the Sacred and Ephemeral* is the text I shift the critical onus to, and this essay will unravel by and by the necessity for such an introduction.

I really do not know if C.P. Surendran's stand-alone books *Canaries on the Moon, Portraits of the Space We*

Occupy and *Posthumous Poems* can be roped into the pattern of trilogy, or, for that matter, Kamala Das' well-known volumes, but here we have Kiriti Sengupta who is bold enough to make a clean breast of his three books, viz., *My Glass of Wine*, *The Reverse Tree*, and *Healing Waters Floating Lamps* as a trilogy titled *Dreams of the Sacred and Ephemeral*. Trilogies in Indian English novels are common, we can foremost thank Mr. Amitav Ghosh for that, but for a trilogy in Indian English poetry, Kiriti Sengupta deserves mention, and also my extended hand for a warm handshake. Hailing from the Dionysia festivals of ancient Greece, a trilogy is a set of three works of art that are connected. And the manner in which Kiriti establishes his connections in the three books is essentially romantic. A very subjective Kiriti upholds his trilogy with a perfect combination of mimesis, pragmatism, expression and objectivity. It becomes indeed necessary to state that we found such romantic balance earlier only in Keats. But here, Kiriti is an Indian; and can Indians come anywhere close to Keats? Well, let it remain unanswered, for such magic questions may conjure up debates of counter-orientalist natures. But I suddenly feel the need to mention M. H. Abrams' *The Mirror and the Lamp* in this context, where the critic shows how *"until the Romantics, literature was typically understood as a mirror reflecting the real world in some kind of mimesis; whereas for the Romantics, writing was more like a lamp: the light of the writer's inner soul spilled out to illuminate the world."* Kiriti does just that, in the Indian context, but with his defined Indian ethos.

Apart from Keats' other Odes, when I first read "Ode to a Nightingale," "Ode on a Grecian Urn" and "Ode to Autumn" at the graduation level of the University of Calcutta, I felt that in a romantic bid Keats was as if walking into different studios — of music, sculpture, and nature respectively — in a quest for the ideal. And I felt that he stood refuted by the *"deceiving elf"* of a Nightingale and the *"Cold Pastoral"* of a Grecian Urn as he sought for the ideal of *their* peripheries. But the ephemeral Autumn [through its Autumnal decay] offered him solace by stripping off his notions of the conventional ideal, by giving an 'outside / beyond' meaning to his transcendental moment of poetry by saying, *"Think not of them, thou hast thy music too—"* I shall relate how Kiriti does just this in his trilogy *Dreams of the Sacred and Ephemeral* and create a graph of his essentially 'Indian' romantic triad. Just as the Nightingale and the Grecian Urn flung Keats back to his prosaic and mundane reality after allowing momentary participation with the fleeting 'ideal,' so is it with Kiriti's *My Glass of Wine* which he gets sentimentally spongy on, and *The Reverse Tree* which allows him a momentary glimpse of the ideal's obliqueness and 'otherness.' They are more prose than poetry, and they define for him the prosaic. Finally, *Healing Waters Floating Lamps* allows him his share of the ideal that can be realized from earth-bound reality's fold, much like Keats' Autumn, and also keeps ajar for him the doors of the ephemeral and the beyond [the 'outside' to].

Over the years expressions have changed their forms, and we can anticipate a postmodern author to reflect the Keatsian psyche but with a new expression altogether. For him, Keatsian versification might recede to the backdrop and he might refrain from stating his poetic anxiety by not beginning with "My heart aches…" [c.f. "Ode to a Nightingale"]. He might reinstate his faith on "Bacchus and his pards" [Ibid.] but in an altogether new "glass of wine." That is what Kiriti does in *My Glass of Wine*, in fine prose and verse well-knit to bring about a profound effect on the minds of the readers. Spurred by his unbranded "homemade wine" he feels "spiritually baptized" and craves for his "olden golden days" in the poem titled "Blood Related." He flouts religions and territories but not divinity, and thereby banks upon a "blood relation" which for him is "impeccable" as the "legacy goes on" between "Father and son," — time past and time present. Interestingly, he chooses for his *Dreams of the Sacred and Ephemeral*, the iconic kingfisher instead of the nightingale to don the cover page with. It is a speckled and barred black and white kingfisher, or in common terms, the Asian 'Pied Kingfisher' of the species *Ceryle Rudis*. Here Kiriti retains his Asiatic ethos. "Its black and white plumage, crest and the habit of hovering over clear lakes and rivers before diving for fish make it distinctive," says Linnaeus in the landmark 10th edition of his *Systema Naturae* [1758]. Kiriti deliberately chooses the bird over the Keatsian nightingale to define his pursuit for truth all the better, instead of leaving it in the mould of the Grecian Urn's paradox of "Beauty is truth, truth beauty." He dives into remembrance and comes out with "the story of his watching movies" in his beak, in the poem titled "Namesake." Emotions flood his brain as "Rains." His first book clearly projects how the "rains" 'dampen' "the [poetic] interior and cannot be seen." Such agony received by him from his "glass of wine" prepares the poet to try his situation under *The Reverse Tree*.

It is evident that Kiriti's pathos of poetic anxiety and poetic predicament heighten and worsen in *The Reverse Tree*. He finds himself "In Others' Shoes" and starts reflecting on the lopsidedness of it. He perhaps finds himself in, and is all too scared by, poetic stasis and tries to pathetically justify 'mimicry' saying— "Mimicry is an art, if practiced wisely [to] ... entertain others and uplift the mood of ... acquaintances. Not ... injuring anyone's sentiments ... [by showcasing] your performer spirit." It is evident that Kiriti is using something of a near-sarcasm on his own poetic, creative persona which urgently requires flinging off borrowed garbs. He posits the very essential question of the creative process of 'unlearning to re-learn' in order to be able to create afresh instead of mimicking anyone or anything. He addresses this issue through "Long ... A Metaphor" where he urges an everyman thus — "Please spend a little more from your wallet, and ask your stylist if the wig you intend to buy resembles the texture and style of your lost hair. If you aren't careful, your audience will soon locate your fake affair with the hair." He admits it point-blank a few lines later where he states, "As I wrote these lines I visualized a poet with long hair that was kept tied by an elastic band." Kiriti has a fine semi-bald middle and wears his hears short-cropped on the sides till the tips of the sideburns. So the poet in question is not Kiriti himself, but Kiriti upholds the plight of mimics in general, and keeps his fingers crossed lest he too has to bask in such poetic stasis. He is introspective throughout and in a later line humbly admits to himself— "I have failed to become a poet." He addresses this 'crisis' of the self and the anti-self in "Crisis" itself and reiterates the probable existence of 'the other' in the very poetic psyche of the creative persona where, for the poet, "*the sun has dared to surface / ... playing both / as she, and a he toy.*" Again, he experiences a "Jet Lag" in his "flight poetry," is not himself appreciative of it, but he thanks his readers for "flying with *The Reverse Tree.*"

The projected differences of sentiments, introspection and sarcasms between *My Glass of Wine* and *The Reverse Tree* reach profundity and spiritual-ethereal calm in *Healing Waters Floating Lamps*. As the title suggests, it conjures up in the Indian mind the very essence of the sacred evenings of *Har ki Pauri Ghat* in Haridwar, or, for that matter, the *Dasashwamedha Ghat* in Varanasi, where believers float prayer-lamps on the sacred Ganga to illumine the later-lives of their loved ones who have reached the ideal land of the spirit, where bodies do not matter, and body-banes automatically stand healed. Kiriti gives the glimpse of the ideal in a frame of eternal flux, just as Keats had done in "Ode to Autumn" upholding the powers of flux, decay, natural order of seasons and the promise of a new awakening in spiritual regeneration. He dedicates the book to Tagore and sees "Beyond the Eyes" to "*draw a circle in the water.*" This circle is as much seen as it is unseen. It is there as much as it is not. It is present in its absence and absent in its presence. This circle is matter and anti-matter alike. Here Kiriti takes "*a dip*," just as Keats had come to terms with, or had compromised with, nature's studio in "Ode to Autumn." And in "After Bath," he has already paid his "*first obeisance.*" His "Evening Varanasi" clearly reaches the fire of his Hindu ethos and philosophy [and the fire of his verses] to the ethereal through water; but fire and water are contraries. In defense of his poesy he sums up saying, "*Water here is not the fire-extinguisher, but / The flames ascend through water / / Prayers reach the meditating Lord.*" The poet deliberately retains an oscillation between a dream of the ideal-spiritual and the reality of existence. And, he leaves this collection open ended with a searching take on what 'should be,' and thereby refutes mere earth-bound spirituality in "In Dusty Feet" saying — "*God remained thumb-sized with dusty feet.*"

Note:

The part of the essay-title in double quotation marks has been taken from the last line of John Keats' "Ode to a Nightingale."

The 'Self' is the Surveyor — an Analyst
P C K Prem

Kiriti is not obscure or burlesque and yet rhythmic mirroring of age, times and experiences, baffles. You realize life in the process of breaking down with a thud, for he strikes with a twist but it rarely happens. He intimidates and coaxes, and obliquely entertains with a proviso that defies brain and serenity. It is the aptitude to hold firmly opposing ideas, images and linguistic arsenal so that you create disjointed memoirs in an exciting intellectual quest.

Mix up of various genres of writing is autobiographical in tone and tenor, at times musical and then, suddenly it is strident. Surprisingly, journalistic phrases give aromatic freshness that throw tip-offs of intrinsic propensity to glorify 'self' in overturning mode of thought where everything turns arcane and you interlace fragile absurdities with realities of life and initiate dawdling breach of what life is made of amidst anarchic rage of times.

He delights as he goes to lanes of the past and resurrects experiences and offers aesthetic pleasure. He is not isolated but involvement also casts shadows on truth. It is not the content or the style he adopts or the personas he depicts, it's the vast landscape of simple experiences he wishes to immortalize through ordinary men and incidents while sustaining naturalness. Kiriti loves to celebrate an excellent technique of good writing with a superb blend of emotional and academic content. He raises questions on poetry, prose, narration and idiom he employs where disquieting newness is manifest.

He writes fast, and thoughts crowd the mind. If one catches hold of the cadence and axiom, he ensures pleasure in poetry and prose. Naturally, it requires certain discipline as it invites the readers to reflective criticism at the end of each argument but it is not important that you agree what he says. It is sufficient that you enjoy and this hidden joy is integral to what he writes. An enlightening statement on life and experiences with apparently tenuous but strong philosophical undertones is what awakens laid-back consciousness.

The 'self' analyzes and explores interesting truths selectively, and Kiriti Sengupta does it in distinctive artistic genres because 'the self' is the motivating force. Kiriti surprises with slick, glossy and nicely published books. The first look amazes, the language baffles, the thought content raises questions and you sit quietly, stare blankly and then, probe into what the author wishes to say. It happens because he puts a spectrum of colors on lexis at multiple layers of comprehension, and still the real meaning eludes if you are not conscious of the art of inveigling an astute artist invokes. Undoubtedly, it satisfies intrinsic sensibilities but at the same time, it arouses the reader to get up and start moving with each line and suddenly, he feels ensnared and that is how you get introduced to Kiriti's poetry and prose.

My Glass of Wine startles a reader with its freshness of approach to literary art but at times, he digs grooves so deep that a reader is puzzled. Autobiographical in nature, it is interesting for its treatment of ordinary incidents and encounters with nearby people of different social grades. Kiriti is frank, candid and astutely selective in the choice of incidents and people, appears cautious while describing flaws and strong points of men and woman he meets. Not often he is obvious in revealing negative persona. It is the first impression he gives. *My Glass of Wine* is readable and one can just do it in a single sitting. You travel with the author and enjoy stunning construction of lines whether prose or poetry.

Poetic lines are magical. Characters he depicts and experiences he shares, just fascinate, and it looks quite possible a reader may identify with certain experiences, may be fragmentary, fractured and loosely connected many a time. Kiriti has a technique that amazes. It looks a small book but it is big…and so do not pick up casually. It has a few solemn territories of philosophy, genuine feelings for man and humanity, caring attitude toward human bonds and love for culture and a bit of spirituality; and a secular approach to religions without hang-ups. Why and how eats up nearly thirty pages but the argument does not irritate.

The author speaks of life and living in just eight chapters. In "As I Traversed," he, though a lethargic reader, yet recalls how in 1995, he got interested in Bengali literature through girlfriend Bhaswati, who became his future wife. Love with literature began with Tagore's novel *Shesher Kobita* and then he never looked back. Despite initial difficulties he did not relent and very soon forays into poetry added spice to his zeal for reading. Literature is a source of entertainment he feels. He looks into varied features of poetry and other genres. Poetry is a gist of human experiences for him. It is everything and if you act like fuel you are perfect. *My Glass of Wine* talks of his days when he studied Dentistry. Through a soul mate, a lady-friend, he visited a Church and learnt many soul-filling shades of Bible and an all embracing humanism of Christianity. 'Blood Related' is a little verse that speaks of joining link -Hinduism, Quran, Bible and humanism.

You and I
The Father and son
The legacy goes on.
Inevitable-impeccable,
Blood relation...

"My sister's *Bhaiya*" makes interesting reading where he talks of names and how Indians love and adore names ... and people are not averse to drawing heavily from scriptures and books of import. In "Southern Affiliation," he narrates experiences of a visit to Chennai where he attended a workshop. He talks of teachers, teachers' counsel and words of wisdom and in between a mention of Krishna and Arjuna gives it a different orientation. He also goes to Udupi. So many wise men and so naturally, verses like "The Encyclopedia," "Market," and "Clarity" come out of Kiriti's pen, a tribute in gratitude to mentors and memories of places. In a verse "Clarity," he says, "*I do not miss the aroma nowadays. / The smell was so organic; / I do wonder why / we never termed milk aromatic!*" "Rains" for him means a feeling when he feels lost, lost anywhere amidst humdrum of life and then, as usual he falls into reflections — some appear relevant, a few are just for pleasure with a few blank verses.

They are siblings;
the older fetches rain, while
the other burns my train.
They keep on hugging
enticing my hunger and greed.

The above lines from "Clips" recount little experience from different stages of life including childhood and family. The last segment "My Master and the Cover" talks about the making of design of the book, its appropriateness and so on...but when Kiriti talks of his guru Dr Ashoke Kumar Chatterjee, he is nostalgic and true and is indebted to him in many ways. It is good to acknowledge contribution of teachers, a rare characteristic in students. Guru's approach to life is meaningful and so essential in the contemporary context and that makes the section beautiful.

When one contemplates on transitory issues, these appear redundant but then, these are hazards of autobiographical writing. It is difficult to be judicious, impartial and ruthless in personalized writing, and therefore, truth and facts do become casualties even without wanting but I find it needs extraordinary courage and intellectual honesty to recognize 'the self', a man rarely reveals and in efforts to allow a man within to grow, he goes beyond formalistic approach.

The Reverse Tree makes interesting reading and one ought to be cautious for each little snippet leads to a quizzical situation and before you arrive at a possible import another grilling situation leaves a dent. Men are 'seedy' and 'non-flowery' but are not active, and a woman for him is the server and that way he pays tributes to womanhood. At a few places, words carry pragmatic strains of irony. In a slightly individualistic style, he interprets the roles men and women play in society, which one often ignores. 'Anti–clock' and 'In others' Shoes' are ordinary experiences but its ornamentation puzzles with a truth one never cares to imagine. He consciously constructs opposing situations to obtain delight many fail to make out.

In an autobiographical vein, Kiriti looks at each moment and defines its traditional meaning and purpose. It has linguistic beauty that at times, irritates and you sit down to reflect and then, thump heads. 'Crisis' relates a few charming but banging encounters Kiriti confronts. Quite ordinary but itching and memorable without intent to convey meaning if one so enquires. He contemplates on man, woman, sex, transgender, gay culture, Vedic views on sex and then, through Lara and Sumit, he talks implicitly about personal relations and relations that society dictates. Anguish of Lara and Sumit's desertion of Lara make a poignant narration and in between, elegiac purring grants fine time. He speaks of Lara's agony –

I was hesitant, you know, I never said goodbye
signs are private, and I keep my eyes
open around the clock!
Chirantan, a nephew appears in 'Jet Lag' and a few oblique poetic lines on the black and white act as brainteasers...a secular outlook? Scrappy and unconnected thoughts and emotions, at times, are incorporated to give expression to inherent feelings otherwise lying dormant because of certain reasons. Autobiographical treatment looks anomalous if not odious. Kiriti is aware what he wishes to say and he does it in an indirect mechanism. 'Reversal...Reverse All' reveals thought pattern and philosophic construction the author wants people to know. He talks of Hindus, Muslims and Christians and the scriptures. The *Geeta* appears close to the idea of life and existence

and then, he picks up a few verses and interprets in contemporary context.

He talks of *Geeta* to define what it means when it tells about Master/Teacher. To him mother is the greatest teacher and probably this is the essence he wants to convey. When he quotes a verse (XV, 1) from the *Geeta*, he appropriately makes a mention of banyan tree. Its roots go upward, branches down ...and that way it justifies the title '*The Reverse Tree*'.

Kiriti experiments with experiences, persons he meets and tries to derive meaning he desires. It is just a sharing, not a message. You think you wasted time and energy but next moment, you realize, well, it was good to sit and think of life through what you do and do not mean it. If it lacks unity and rationality then can anyone find coherence and reason in life and existence? He is plainspoken and hits you not very hard but questions you on vital facets of life, which you fail to listen and that is the strength of this tiny book. He writes little but he evinces faith in literature as a piece of art and fundamental constituent of existence of man and culture.

Celebrating and Reliving Experiences offer perceptive inkling to life in current situation in Kiriti Sengupta *Healing Waters Floating Lamps*. It is lively but taxing, engaging but ambiguous at times. It resurrects experiences of the inner and outer world vividly. He is a subtle player of words conveying compound meanings with several layers and images, and yet confuses with a distinctly teasing vagueness. You need incisive and piercing intellect to understand. To go beyond what eyes perceive is risky –

I reach the sky
While I draw a circle in the water
Looking at the image
I take a dip

Eyes touch sky is an experience and offers a chance to go beyond and beyond and again, to draw lines on water creates crowds of images, visible and invisible but only to be felt. It is the ultimate dissolving of 'self'. He hints at duality and oneness of Creation and Created beings. What images! A prayer to Sun god allude to an inner struggle and gives signals for enjoying a few moments where spirits take you to the eternity and the unknown, for the imagination of the poet goes wild, and nevertheless the agitating mind to probe into the mystery of life hangs on, and at another level, floating lamps become curriers of prayers that would grant deliverance, and the simile 'flames ascend through water' reinforces the belief in the unsteadiness of mind and heart but gives intimations of continuing journey to the infinite. A wish to unite with the indefinite mysterious presence surfaces in 'River of Tears', and the lines 'Reach the void, and see the cage' in 'Unravel' speak symbolically of contemporary confusion. 'fast food, lawsuits' and 'spiritual pursuits' amid dusty and empty front(?) are apparently vague and hence, give rise to many meanings, and forceful puzzlements (?).

'In Dusty Feet' a sense of washing out of ego is dominant as a tiny grain of dust invokes prayers and deference with a fragile quietness. Flights to the unknown are visible in the eyes of a yogi. May be he hints at racial thoughts (Color Code) lying dormant in the subterranean dark depths of mind he continuously digs. Mystic probes confound the lyricist and he stuns –

This is not all about
Day-light photography
This is rather reaching you
As if you're the destination... (Sun)

A mechanical function touches faith and then, he turns agnostic when he observes – Rituals of self reflection end /With gods and goddesses /The river turns pregnant' 55 and so the last lines give a huge shock to understanding and asks readers to stay alert as he begins another distinct flight to the indefinite –

You spin and continue to swirl
Since periods unknown. (Since Time Unknown)

It appears poet lingers on with intrinsic perplexity because colorful rambling dance and imagery at times, teases readers. In fragmentary voyages, one naturally observes that the poet is not steady, never roosts on a single idea but clutches in a fist so many messy and chaotic feelings, impressions and thoughts and reaches nowhere and yet he wants readers to walk into the inner world of foggy 'self' with shadows in abundance while on route creates an engaging lyrical world. Beautiful photographs in black and white allure and characteristically convey many meanings of a frenzied and shaky world in an age of uncertainty as if. He is skillful in the use of language and depicts characters' qualities and instantly one finds him depersonalized in describing experiences but it is a transitory phase. He demonstrates experiential and experimental proclivity even toward different characters, no doubt without apparent prejudice, but still gets dissolved in 'the self' and there ends the disconnection. As expected, he does not adhere to one ultimate meaning he wishes to convey through the text but one finds deconstruction quite active and it offers varied meanings, some so clear on surface and a few meanings seem conditional. In the final analysis, it makes an interesting reading.

Extracting the tooth; extracting the truth!
U Atreya Sarma

As soon as I received *The Unheard I* from Kiriti Sengupta on August 8, 2013, I pored over the sleek volume which gripped the attention right from its very title, right from its first page. What then is this book about? Well, it's an olio of the author's (as well as others') personal and inter-personal experiences, incidents, episodes, cameos, observations, perceptions, generalizations and principles underlying the art of literary writing, brought out in a uniquely creative and seamless way. And it was done almost in a jiffy – from conception to execution.

When the state of Oklahoma (USA) was devastated by a tornado as recent as in May 2013, a virtual international literary group – *Indies in Action* – decided in June to bring out an anthology to give some relief to the victims with its proceeds. And the international anthology – *Twist of Fate* (ToF) - comprising 200 pages of writes by 50 authors was ready in print as early as July 4, edited by Stephen L Wilson and published by Navigator Books. Just two weeks thereafter, on July 18, Kiriti's book - *The Unheard I* - was out, making known the hitherto "unknown... fact that the author has been merging the different modes of writing, the poetic and the nonfictional, against the backlash of his expertise and memoirs in journalism," to quote from the Foreword by hülya yilmaz (who never capitalizes her name), a professor of German Language and Literature and Comparative Literature & Turkish, Pennsylvania State University, USA.

Indies in Action is a site of "charity anthologies designed to donate all proceeds to the victims of various tragedies. It is a way for authors to contribute their work and compassion to those who need it the most," and the word "Indies" according to a telephonic clarification by Kiriti stands for "Independents."

Now let's go over the vignettes in the book.

Though Kiriti gave Don Martin the absolute editing freedom, Don, in his Editorial Note, says that he found little need of it for "The language in the book is actually better than common US English," even as it is Kiriti's debut book. Not favoring "full-blown Americanization," and believing that "part of the beauty of the English language" owes it to the "character or the flavor of the author, regardless of his native language." He has effected only a few changes to ensure that a "Western English-speaker" doesn't have any trouble in reading and understanding the book. What appears in it "may not be strictly American English," he affirms, only to ask "but why should it be?" *The Unheard I* contains some poetry – in English original as well as in translation from Bengali, where Don says he hasn't really touched it save a few punctuation and grammatical changes. Don ascribes the minimal editorial intervention to what he calls the first rule of editing poetry - "No matter what you do, you never, ever change any poetry." And he elucidates: "...poetry is such a tightly-written literary form that if you change even one word you can sometimes change the entire meaning of the poem."

Kiriti, in his Introduction, honestly shares with the readers that in fact the two English poems he submitted for ToF came to be rejected by Stephen Wilson for one of them was "too abstract to fit with the mood of the anthology, while the other had strong sexual connotations that might offend the readers." At the same time two short stories by his friend Prabir Roy translated by Kiriti from Bengali came to be accepted. It was some consolation. Then on Stephen's suggestion Kiriti sent in his replacements. A short autobiographical sketch, 'As I Traverse,' was readily accepted. Thus Kiriti has proved that life sails, and also it sells, in his own words.

Kiriti's joy was doubled when his other submission – a poem in Bengali in translation by his friend Ranadeb Dasgupta - had also been accepted though after some hurdles. While Ranadeb had appraised the original as a "fantastic composition," Stephen commented on its translated version: "I really don't understand this poetry, I will post it in the group, will pin it and if any of the fellow poets can make me understand the hidden imagery, I promise that I would publish it in the anthology." Thankfully, the poem did win the group's approval. This incident shows that if you have the real merit it is bound to come to the fore, that the perception of appreciation differs from reader to reader, and that every poet has their readers.

As a freelance journalist since 1998 Kiriti has "always enjoyed interviewing celebrities, performers, and artists," and *ToF* had stimulated him to interview its contributors and ask "intriguing questions." While the dentist in Kiriti extracts many a tooth, the journo in him is keen to "extract the truth."

An interesting take on poetry vs news is here. When Kiriti in his interview asked Jon Tribble whether "poetry could communicate only with the poets," the latter quotes: "It is difficult / to get the news from poems / yet men die miserably every day / for lack / of what is found there," from the 1955 poem 'Asphodel, That Greeny Flower' by William Carlos Williams.

Kiriti rues that the editors of literary work don't get due recognition for their contribution and are "never given the tag of a contributor." This point is, however, debatable since he hasn't substantiated his observation. Viewing a literary journal or compilation as the product of team work, Don Martin responds: "There are the cover artists, the book designer, and all sorts of behind-the-scenes people. Someone even has to select the font!" Well, a humble editor could say so, but never our strutting Indian movie heroes — who are given to hogging all the limelight and usurping the lion's share of the budget.

On the question of translation, Kiriti demurs that "translators are frequently looked down upon and we appreciate only the original writers for the work!" In this context, he gives the impression of Ranadeb who has translated his Bengali poem into English for ToF. Ranadeb explains:

"Translation is a tough journey as well as important too. Not only because we can taste literature of other languages which we don't know but also for the reason that a successful translation may convey so silently the inner depth of writing to the readers of other languages. It implicates the efficiency of the translator. A good translator must have literary sense and ability to follow the hidden tune of the original writing... Probably, a suggestion plays in our minds that a translator is not the creator. I believe that there could be no translation without trans-creation. A translator, when translates, trans-creates simultaneously because there is no such language which can express the feel of another language totally. I must conclude that the view about translators should be changed right now."

To me it appears that there can be no single opinion on the observation that translators don't get due recognition.

Kiriti's observation that poetry is a wonderful medium to reach out to not only the literature lovers but also God - corroborates the Indian experience! Traditionally, not just literature but every art is dedicated to the divine in India which "boasts the lineage of the Yogis, and Sages". Rooted as he is in this ethos, Kiriti wishes due recognition for spiritual lyrics and poetry. Devotional poetry "artistically conveys our... desires, prayers, demands and frustrations to the Lord." But this type of poetry is "not well regarded in the world of literature," he highlights. Though "much has been written on Yoga... little research has been done... on the influences of yoga in English literature," he adds.

Kiriti, who was initiated into Kriyayoga by Yogacharya Dr Ashoke Kumar Chatterjee in 2008, informs us that Swami Yukteshwar Giri, a prominent disciple of Yogiraj Lahiree Mahasaya, did a yogic interpretation of *The Bible*. Later on Paramahansa Yogananda, foremost disciple of Yukteshwar Giri and author of the spiritual bestseller, *Autobiography of a Yogi*, propagated Kriyayoga in the United States. On a personal note, I recall having bought my copy of this book as well as its Telugu version *Oka Yogi Atma Katha* on June 11, 1994, though I am eons behind Kiriti in praxis.

Asked about her view on "spirituality, religion and God," which to Kiriti are synonymous, Dr hülya yilmaz cited her favorite quotation: "Those who say religion has nothing to do with politics do not know what religion is." And these are the words of Mahatma Gandhi. And hasn't Einstein said too: "Science without religion is lame; Religion without science is blind?"

When the literati of different nationalities and languages as in the *Indies in Action* group is able to come together for a larger common cause, it strikes us: why can't leaders and preachers of different religions across the world come similarly together for a better humanity?

Linda Bonney Olin of USA from the *Indies in Action* brings in an analogy. When the great hymns of yore are able to inspire people long after their creators passed away, why can't the poets "write something that would significantly touch hearts," in a similar way?

Kiriti showcases a poem of his — "The Unheard" as an example of one that has appealed to the general readers of poetry as well as God-lovers. Here it is in its translation from Bengali by Gopal Lahiri, a friend of Kiriti:

> That road is still wet even today—
> Fasting though; the journey that started
> Ended in curse.
> It was all dark, sudden gust of wind
> Arrived the rain clouds,
> Favorite leather shoes,
> Salty smell in
> Godly wind.
> Felt the bliss
> Had a bath near well
> Awaken, Thy Name!
> Awaken, The Heaven.
> Neither love nor cuddle
> Taut breast flirts,
> That road is still wet even today…

How God's grace can be like the proverbial slip between the lip and the cup, unless the devotee is single-minded and self-disciplined, is brought home in a tongue-in-cheek manner in the following lines from the poem, 'Stairs.' Penned originally in Bengali by Kiriti, here is its English rendition by Shishir Kumar Roy, a senior sub-editor of *Ananda Bazar Patrika*.

> Since my college days, my dinner ends around
> One at night. Mother keeps awake, awaits me,
> Without taking her food. Says she, 'Why don't
> You cut down these hang-outs?'
> Rules, such mess of rules cause my headache.
> God arrives at the wee hours of morn whilst the
> Alarm is set at nine for me.

Veering back to the arena of translation, Kiriti tells us that he never self-translates his Bengali works lest he might "get biased as normally happens when a writer translates his/her own compositions." He is "pretty serious" while translating any literary piece, but then he translates the works of others only.

While there are many who would presume, and for good reason, that a lot of people idle and fritter away their time on social networking sites, there is always an exception with creative and dynamic netizens like Kiriti who have put it to good and constructive use – to display their literary merit, to network with unseen and unknown people across the world for a meaningful and edifying friendship - culminating in a moving philanthropic gesture.

In conclusion, I vouchsafe: I've enjoyed reading this book to the hilt for there are many aspects in it I can personally relate to — being an editor, poet, writer and translator of sorts myself, as also a believer in yoga, spiritualism and religion.

Kiriti Sengupta — a Pioneering Genius in Poetizing Yogic Science

Dalip Kumar Khetarpal

When a dentist, a man of science, forays into the world of literature and eventually into the world of spirit, it would betoken his completeness as a man. Strangely, the slender volume has voluminous substance and is marked by rare originality. Kiriti has definitely carved a niche for himself in the literary world by authoring *The Unheard I* seemingly with a view to be properly heard. The catchy title, doubtless, caught my attention, though on going through the book I saw something different — interviews, translations, episodes, yogic sciences, philosophy, mysticism, spiritualism and a host of diverse experiences — all perhaps combined to make Kiriti heard who seemed unheard hitherto. Suppressed or hidden emotion often takes its toll. Hence, a writer often sees that his unique or intense thought is heard and feelings registered, just to feel relieved and satisfied — a flow of pent up thoughts and feelings often eases the heart of its unhealthy burden. However, Kiriti's novel ideas are underliners emphasizing the strength of his feelings, thoughts and beliefs. But I'm sure, his diligence, creative ability and passion for literary creations will soon make him shine like a star in the firmament of literature.

If I don't sound paradoxical, I must admit that I'm only spiritual and not religious. As such, Kiriti's poetry, being somewhat religious in nature, does not dovetail very well with my psyche, though I won't deny that its spiritual aspects fascinate me. Further, though I'm bereft of sound knowledge of religion and required background of yogic sciences, I must still confess that I felt illuminated by his poetry, albeit inexplicably. I'm also broad and liberal minded enough to recognize and appreciate the different perception, outlook, ideology and views presented by him at least for its spiritually lyrical melody and other stylistic beauties emanating from his divine soul and also characterizing his own and his translated works. His unprecedented humanity could be seen in his being an integral part of IIA that evolved into a charitable anthology, *Twist of Fate* [*ToF*]. The optimist Kiriti sees his initial rejection of two poems by Stephen Wilson, the editor of the anthology, as only a minor deficiency on his part that could be easily done away with. So, as expected, he tried again and did succeed in his second attempt which made it to the anthology. Had he been a pessimist, he would have ascribed his failure to some lasting deficiency that could never be removed. I'm sure, had he failed even in his second attempt, he would still have gone in for the third. However, *ToF* has provided abundant scope to vent his immense humanity through liberally contributing his divine lyrics to the anthology for garnering funds for tornado hit, marooned, distressed and wretched victims in Oklahoma.

Kiriti's own original composition in English is illuminating and thought provoking. One experiences the feel of salvation through the infinite agony, suffering and sacrifice of Christ:

...carrying oneself
Crucify is Christ-filled
I remember and mind turns candle lit.

The mindlessness and insensitivity of the world which has been witnessed since ages is seen today also:

They pinned it before, will do that now again
No arrangements of incenses though!

The lines are really pathetic, excruciatingly painful, heart-rending and delineate how great saints and sages have been ruthlessly treated and tortured since ages making "Life and God" more distant from human ken.

"Communion," based on scriptural verse, explains all that exists within the human body. The poet's projection of how yogic science achieves a mystical form is interestingly mystical. The poem unfolds that *Shat-Chakra* is perceptible along the spinal cord of the human body. While the base i.e. *Muladhara* is at the base adjacent to the anus, *Sahasrara* is at the head. Energy that is represented through a female snake, *Kula Kundalini* ascends from *Muladhara* to *Sahasrara* to materialize the communion which when effected, a human is transformed into a yogi whose body becomes so divine that it could even be equated with God.

"Stairs" that emerged from *Patanjal Yoga Sutras* is known as "Asthanga Yoga" as it carries the following eight limbs

1. *Yama* [means, s*anyam*, restraint. *Yama* is often wrongly considered as *Yama-Raj*, the god of Death!]
2. *Niyam* [means, discipline]
3. *Asana* [means, posture]
4. *Pranayama* [yogic breathing, and please, don't mix this up with the conventional breathing exercises as shown in TV channels.]
5. *Pratyahara* [spontaneous withdrawal from the outer world]
6. *Dharana* [means, idea]
7. *Dhyana* [means, keeping engrossed ... this is not synonymous with meditation. Meditation is a verb, while *Dhyana* is noun!]
8. *Samadhi* [means, ultimate union with God]

The poet was honest and realistic enough to make a mention of only seven limbs in the poem since he has practically experienced all these seven stages of spiritual development. But as he has not gone through the eighth i.e. *Samadhi*, he has not made even an imaginary mention of it. As such, the poem emerges from the direct experience of the poet. Now, mystic experience undergone by saints and sages when really experienced by Kiriti one can well presume that he could even be canonized like great saints of the *Holy Bible* one fine day. Another unique aspect of the poem is the subtle and humorously artistic juxtaposition of the earthly and spirituality:

...then a couple of hours in prayer, so
Irritating! My morning sleep goes haywire
...today's 'Ekadashi' a religious fortnightly
The mammary glands of the cows are dry, oil-free
And heavy with pain

Despite Kiriti's rigorous training in translation, the poet, if humble, must admit that he deliberately translated only those substantial works which were appealing to him and which according to him should attract wider readership. In view of this, it was wise of him to have rendered Mr. Suprakash Pramanik's "Bonfire" into English. The poem is abstract but highly metaphorical and metaphysical in nature:

'crystals' 'of' 'sentiments' have been 'made' into 'dust' to be further diffused 'in the air'. One can't smell it for 'the sky' is 'so huge'.

The poet's translation of Ranadeb Dasgupta's "The Cycle" is also praiseworthy. The poem is terse and a lot of wisdom is compressed into a small space:

Break it
Abolish it further
Particles have their own character

His simple but realistic perception of how and why should one

*await the absolute
around the soil and sky*

When while coming

*a bit closer to the earth
...the grass, water, flower and blood*

One could easily have a tryst with the absolute, the Almighty. The uncertainty of even the final truth is illustrated through subtle analysis:

*Even the complete fetches illusive touch at times
those decent lies.*

Sumita's Nandy's "Sleep" translated by Kiriti is a purely psychological poem. Sleep is just a periodic state of muscular relaxation, low metabolic rate, and suspended state of consciousness wherein a person is mainly unresponsive to any event in the given environment. In this poem, the poet's focus shifts from normal to disturbed sleep. Starting with normal sleep that

*Keeps on changing with every passing day
The color of sleep
Dream surfaces as occurs sleep*

The focus shifts to daydreaming which often occurs during depression or elation:

All around the day
Dreams come hidden like haunted nights

Followed by a weird:

...Connection between
The dead mountain with the spoiled moonlight

This is further followed by metaphorically telling lines:

...emptying rice-plate alike
The moon half

Finally, how the overpowering sleep could also be drowned in dreams and how dreams drive a person crazy are deftly and artistically expressed:

Huge sleep was in dreams
Yesterday
...And in sleep
A crazy night

I somehow feel that a kind of sleep disorder called dyssomnia has been alluded to in the said lines. Dyssomnia is associated with disturbances of sleep patterns, involving various disturbances in the quality, amount, and timing of sleep. Though I've not read the original poem, I feel that it must be mesmerizing and Kiriti's translation, as evident, is also mesmerizing in it's own way though some nuances of some ideas, I think, have not been properly captured.

The translation of Uttam Kumar Dutta's "Racecourse" by Kiriti is also strikingly effective. The shift from the trivial to the sublime shows psychic evolution of the poet. The poet's bifocal vision becomes glaring after his arrival at the stable from the racecourse when he looks at:

God with sided eyes—
And a little loving you

And also

Resonating audio from the Jockey's whip

Followed by a grim irony:

...race depicting our murderer destiny
Amongst loads of envies and maddening claps
Glooms the brilliance of advancing vigor

These lines are bitterly satirical and deeply meaningful and wrench at the hearts of the readers with their hidden content. At a glance, the poem appears to be a ludicrous mix of the earthly and divine but on further scrutiny, one discovers that it is the sublime, the spirit, the Almighty that triumphs over all that is mundane and earthly. The book concludes with the finest manifestation of the poet's enunciation of his breadth of vision illustrating how all heterogeneities in life are synthesized into a homogenous harmony and how his tryst with the divine has been his long cherished dream and further how 'soul and deity' are inseparable — the most universal concept conceived by man.

A pioneering genius in poetizing yogic science, Kiriti emerges as a rare poet. Through yogic poetry, he has dared to tread the inexplicable labyrinthine path of literature that only the literate few would dare do. But to rise to greater heights, the poet, henceforth, should focus on different subjects and themes that are comprehensible and appealing to a common man.

The Making of a Poet
U Atreya Sarma

Here is an interesting book featuring interviews of three noted Bengali poets by Dr Kiriti Sengupta, a writer cum dentist drawing out their creative processes, literary output and philosophy. He tags each interview with a set of four best poems of the respective poets translated by him. The book is an attempt to address the regret that the 'rich heritage of Bengali poetry' is not showcased for the English-knowing global readership. This position along with his other observation that "we are working on issues that are not conducive to the projection of Bengali poetry to the outer world" holds equally good with the other Indian languages as well.

Joya Mitra, Ranadeb Dasgupta and Suddhasatya Ghosh reveal that they are immensely knowledgeable, learned and incisive with great poetic sensibility. Since their poetries are not "so culture-specific," the author hopes they will "have a universal appeal."

All these poets have a communist background, yet their poetic work or philosophy is uninfluenced by it, rooted in and inspired as they are by ancient Indian literature — *Ramayana, Mahabharata, Bhagavad Gita, Veda*s,

*Upanishad*s, *Purana*s, Sanskrit literature — which they continue to drawn on.

Jailed for four and a half years for her Naxal activities, Joya Mitra has several poetry publications to her credit, and her book – *Hanyaman* – translated as *Killing Days* into English by Shampa Banerjee won an award (Ananda Puraskar, 1991). She also edits a Bengali tri-monthly magazine, *Bhumadhyasagar*. "Not merely a social activist, she works for Mother Nature, and her advocates!"

Then we have Ranadeb Dasgupta, a poet of thirty-five years standing who began to write when he was thirteen. A physics teacher and a CPI activist, he has read a lot of European, Russian and English masters. His *Kobitabela Shono* (Listen Oh Poetic Spell) is "extremely inspiring" to Kiriti, who himself is a bilingual poet both in Bengali and English.

The other one is Suddhasatya Ghosh who has been writing since 1985 when he was eleven. Free of "irrelevant baggage," his poetry reflects his masterful diction. With stints at Doordarshan and ETV, he conducts workshops on elocution, theatre, and stage-plays. Despite huge financial loss due to betrayal and critical health problems he rose like a phoenix and his first novel *Irabati O Du Ekti Chand* was published in *Charyapad*, a Bengali journal in 2003.

While poetry is an "expression of my silent heart" to Joya, Ranadeb declares that his "poems never indulged slogans," and he has "always remained a poet whispering into private ears," rather than being "a poet of the masses." Suddhasatya inherited his political ideology from his father who was "a communist at heart" and read a lot of literature written by communists and their sympathizers. Convinced later on that armed struggle was not the only way, he quit active politics.

Though "Likings keep changing as you proceed with your life," Joya has two special favourite poets: Shankha Ghosh and Bishnu Dey. She says most of Shankha Ghosh's poems have a soft flow, tender yet firm. Steeped in poetry, she finds it mysterious and magical.

'Making of a Poet' is like the cutting of a diamond, observes Ranadeb, and "poetry writing is a kind of mental refraction process ... The waves and rays of running life and surroundings continuously enter my mind and get refracted with varying colours, which I just catch as far as possible and pen down."

If one aspires to be a poet one should study literature, heritage and people to grab their experiences, and "master the art of isolating" oneself "mentally from the environment because a vibrating prism can never produce a good spectrum," advises Ranadeb on whom Jibananda Das and Shankha Ghosh cast a spell.

Curiously, Ranadeb gets touchy on being asked as to why the element of pathos is so crucial in his compositions and to say something about his contemporaries. Nonetheless he brings himself to answer them, the first one rather defensively and the second one unconvincingly. Yet his modest streak surfaces when he confesses: "All my writings... are my conversation with that Omnipotent... I just feel myself a lit-up earthen lamp in the cosmic festival of lights."

Suddhasatya appreciates the work of any poet, even a new comer, where "an idea or word or syntax or philosophy strikes" him. Having an irresistible fascination for *Mahabharata*, he has brought out the first volume of his own version in prose, and is working on the remaining portion. He feels that adequate research has not gone into the study of the epic so much so most of the subsequent renditions are devoid of a demystified, rational and socio-political outlook. This is the most encyclopedic and incredible text where "The great characters are all so human, yet so monumental in their achievements!"

True to the Indian traditions of learning, Suddhasatya is grateful to all his predecessors who "taught me something apiece."

Translation being a vital tool for literary cross-fertilization, it has sufficiently exercised the minds of the three litterateurs. Whatever the approach, the translated text should read clean to the target readers, observes Joya. Kiriti's interview of Ranadeb attributes the non-appreciation of Bengali poetry by the English-speaking readers to want of competent translators. And Suddhasatya pitches in with an apt question: When there are very few Indians with successful writings directly in English, "what can be expected from the translations done from the native languages?" Foreign writers translated into Bengali are read but not vice versa. Perhaps a major part of the answer could lie elsewhere, opines this reviewer. In the first phase of interaction, the Indian literature (in Sanskrit and regional tongues) appealed to the West for its force of nativity, individuality and originality. But eventually with our minds and syllabi getting packed with the massive import of literary genres, schools, content and idiom from the West, our native ethos and creativity has become a casualty. Consequently, our literary output has degenerated into a pathetic imitation of the West. Hence translation or no translation, most of it doesn't make any impact.

Suddhasatya's claim that "W B Yeats first translated the works of Rabindranath" together with its echo in the Foreword by WF Lantry needs to be corroborated since Yeats didn't know Bengali.

In short, *The Reciting Pens* has brought out the psychology and ergonomics of the ink and the pen, of the hand that wields the pen, of the brain that moves the writing finger, of the heart that gives life and soul to the literary creation.

The Reciting Pens — a review
Don Martin

One of the nice things about being an editor and reviewer is I sometimes get to read some books I never would have chosen myself. *The Reciting Pens*, by Kiriti Sengupta, is one example of that. *Pens* is just not a book I would have chosen myself off the shelf of my local bookstore. But I am very happy I read it!

I should probably say up-front that Sengupta is himself a poet of some note. He recently published his first English-language non-fiction, *The Unheard I*. That book, like this one, discusses among other things challenges in translation, especially with respect to poetry. Dr. Sengupta knows his subject, and he knows what he is talking about!

The Reciting Pens is an exploration of Bengali poetry. In his Introduction to the book Sengupta says his goal is to expose English-speaking readers to this unique art form. He further says that Bengali poetry is an under-represented genre in modern literature, and he is probably right about that. The book explores, among other things, the reasons for that, in a quite understandable manner. He presents three notable Bengali poets, all of them contemporary: Joya Mitra, Ranadeb Dasgupta, and Suddhasatya Ghosh. Not only does Sengupta present their poems for our consideration, he also gives us quite a bit of background on the poets. Going even further, Sengupta also interviews the poets, which gives us some context on their work. But more about that later.

Mitra is a poet who says she writes from her "quietude." She explores those silent nooks and crannies we all have in our minds, but we just don't talk about much. Her poetry is eerily haunting, and she writes with a lot of deep meaning. Dasgupta could be considered a dark and brooding poet. An avowed communist, he writes about the ordinary travails and struggles of life, without being overly political. Kiriti finally describes Ghosh as a "lavish" poet. His poems are rich in descriptions of scenery and events, as well as emotions. One thing I like about *Pens* is the poets are all so different, and each offers a different glimpse into their work, and into poetry as a whole.

Poets are funny, because they don't always say what they literally mean. So you don't always know. They use literary tools such as the metaphor to put their meanings across. *The Reciting Pens* allows the reader to go beneath the surface meaning of the poems, and see what they really mean. This is where the background and interviews in *Pens* comes in handy. Having the poet explain their work, in their own words, adds a lot of context, and allows the reader to more correctly interpret their poems. I appreciated that aspect to a book of poetry, which I rarely see.

As with any translated work there are always two risks. The first is the translator must be faithful to the original work. Closely related to this is that the translator must be very careful with his word choices. Sengupta, as the translator, does a masterful job here. In his Introduction to the collection he says right up front he is not going to change much. That's a refreshing change, because I see too many translators who essentially become co-authors. They change so much they are basically rewriting the entire thing. *The Reciting Pens* is pretty much the words the poet actually used, without any modification or editing. This allows the reader to gain the true insight into the poet's intent. The translations in *Pens* are very good, and they are faithful to the poet's original intent.

The other things related to translation are the word choices. There are just some words which don't translate into English very well. This is especially true with a language like Bengali, which is very descriptive (you might even call it "flowery"). Bengali words sometimes have two, three, or even more meanings, all of which are correct. How does the translator know what the poet really meant, what his real intent was? For example, the translation of the Bengali word for "friend" can have any number of meanings, so the translator has to be very careful which English word he picks. Sengupta does a fine job of presenting the translated poetry which is true to the poet's original meanings.

A big bonus to the book are the interviews. Most poets don't like to talk about themselves or their poetry much. Sengupta has a knack for getting them to discuss it. His interview with Dasgupta was a little testy, as I read it.

But Kiriti persisted, and probably got Mr. Dasgupta to reveal more about his work than he ever has before.

This is one of the most interesting things about the book. Sengupta delves deep into the poets. Why do they write what they do? How do their life experiences color their work, and what motivations might they have? For a non-Indian, such as myself, that allows me to read their work and get something meaningful out of it. The three poets profiled could be said to be complex, drawing their inspiration from their spirituality, their political activism, or even just from the beauty of nature or the flow of society. After reading *Pens* I really felt I knew these poets, on more than in just a, "Yeah, I've heard of them" basis. And that, as I see it, is one of the big advantages of the book. Plus, if you enjoy Goethe, Shelley, and Tagore there is plenty there for you to think about.

All-in-all *The Reciting Pens* is a must read for any serious student of poetry, and especially any student of poetic translation. I really admire Sengupta's ability to put it all together — the background, the interviews, and the poems themselves, in such a way that the reader gains deep insights into the poets and their work. It's a rare talent, and you can't go wrong with this book!

My Glass of Wine — a review
Eileen Register

I am not a highly educated professor, though I am an English teacher. I am not a famous author or poet, though I am the author of several novels and have written many poems. I am simply a reader who has been blessed by the opportunity to read a book that is like no other I've read, and being a voracious reader, I have read many.

Understanding the culture and nuances of a place like India is not an easy task for an American, or perhaps anyone who is not from that magical and fascinating country, unless you are fortunate, as I have been, to read Sengupta's latest book, *My Glass of Wine*. The subtitle gives the reader the first hint that this is going to be a very personal book: "It was not only the wine, but that the glass was mine." Through his special way of presenting not only his poetry, but his life and his way of life, the reader is able to grasp the many layers of this man named Kiriti.

As the author presents himself, layer by layer, his poetry captivates one's imagination. A second and third reading reveals even more depth and perception. The preface of the book, written by best-selling American author and editor Don Martin, suggests that one should read each poem before reading the rest of the chapter in which it appears. I tried that for the first couple of chapters, but I found that I enjoyed each poem more once I knew about the cultural backdrop from which it came. Sengupta does a great job in this respect, but he also reveals a bit more of himself as an individual with each explanation, and the poetry is the crowning glory of each chapter. Having a reference from which to embrace the poetry as well as "snapshots" of the author's thoughts makes the poetry infinitely more understandable but does not spoil the beauty of it.

I have known Kiriti Sengupta as a fellow author for over a year via the internet, but it is this book by which I truly began to "know" him. I especially enjoyed the chapter entitled "Rain," in which the bleeding heart of the author is revealed. Through his experiences with love as well as with various ups and downs in life, his romanticism is held up for our view. In the last stanza of the poem, "The Air" he speaks of love in a unique way:

No one knew I worshiped you
With my flaming heart;
No matter if I had a flower white,
You were to float, and fly
Like the passing kite.

[*My Glass of Wine*, pg. 45]

Who among us hasn't loved in vain and felt like that elusive object of our affections floated beyond our reach? In the midst of this romantic notion comes the statement that "love is not a volatile thing, but a strong cerebral affair." He goes further, discussing the setbacks we humans suffer because of love. The first stanza of "Scratches only are human" he compares the hurts received in the course of loving to tiny scratches:

Few beautiful scratches, deep within,
Soft marks, palpable even after months;
No wounds, but tiny scratches brown—
Soothing, mesmerizing in between!

The author explains through his poem entitled "Stay Away" how it feels to lose someone and to be fearful of allowing that person back into one's life only to be engulfed once again in pain:

Feeling you humanly inside
Is indeed a nightmare;
my heart sinks,
and I shrink sidewise…

Feeling you inside in
Not again…not again!

[*My Glass of Wine*, pg. 47]

I have certainly been there, felt that. I suspect anyone who has opened him/herself to love has also felt the pangs of loss and the fear of being hurt again. This and other of the author's poems also apply to times in one's life when things go wrong. Those times are the "rain" in our lives that "dampens the interior and cannot be seen." [pg.44]

I have prattled on about the author's romantic side, perhaps because I, too, am a romantic and write romantic novels and poems, but there is so much more to discover in *My Glass of Wine*. With depth of thought and strong intellect, the author expands his readers' understanding and, perhaps, acceptance of his homeland as well as his religious views and other aspects of himself as a person and as a man. I recommend this book highly as a wonderful way to explore and come to a better understanding of India, the Bengali culture, the unique views espoused about Christianity and how it coalesces with the practice of Yoga, and the man – Kiriti Sengupta.

The Heady Wine of Love and Spirituality
Shernaz Wadia

As I held Dr. Kiriti Sengupta's little book in my hand for the first time, my instant reaction was, "Oh, this shouldn't be too time-consuming." I was right in that it took me just a few hours to read it but it is going to take much longer to savor the delight of the wine in it — the heady wine of love and spirituality; of a curious, contemplative and open mind; a large accepting heart — all embodied in the simple, direct words of the writer that make you enjoy and revel in this intoxicating cocktail of prose and poetry. A delightful experience as we take sips from his glass!

It has already been mentioned by others that this book cannot be pigeonholed. As he says in the preface "When I wrote the manuscript I deliberately wrote down what came into my mind. I never considered what genre my book would fit into." To brand it would be to diminish it. It is a distillation of some momentous pieces ... autobiographical word snapshots, each followed by a poem. This book is Kiriti's humble attempt to take poetry to all book lovers so that it can 'reach its pinnacle again'. With great simplicity he tackles issues of love, spirituality, relationships, the world and nature as he perceives them and brushes them with his poetic sensibility.

He cracks open little drawers and lets us peek into some uplifting moments of his life. The initial glimpse is into his first date with his future wife Bhaswati, which began on a slightly comical note that for him turned into the stepping stone of his literary journey. His wife to-be was quite amused when she asked him about a Rabindranath Tagore novel and he replied that he didn't read poetry at all! Because the novel was *Shesher Kobita*! This honest revelation by Dr. Sengupta at the start of the book immediately endears him to his readers and keeps charming them until the end.

The poet Kiriti was born from the agony of a painful relationship with a friend to whom he addressed his first poem in Bengali. While he says that with all its innumerable functions and facets poetry should also entertain, he believes that true poetry arises out of total consumption of one's being.

Consumption

Consumed time/ like an infant consuming
milk; inevitable/ it remains.
Killed essence of
the eternal soul; and consumed,
Essentially I remain...

The second chapter from which the book takes its title shows us another side of Kiriti as he takes us along on a sacred trek. He is gentle but forthright in the weaving of this tale. We get whiffs of the wine that he imbibes spiritually and are given a peep into that part of his life which was experimental and experiential, culminating into the insightful observation that 'red'— the color of some wines and of blood — is divinely symbolic in Christianity, Tantric Hinduism and Islam. Whereas in Christianity, (to which he received formal baptism after the priest was convinced that he had attained spiritual baptism) 'red wine' is representative of Jesus' godly blood sacrificed for mortals; Tantrics also use alcoholic beverages in their rituals and hold 'red' to be the color of divine power. And so their attire is blood red in hue. With these he compares the Islamic ritual of animal sacrifice — *Qurbani* — and draws the conclusion that 'the elements of blood, power, alcohol and red (are) associated intimately with divinity". "Blood Red", the poem at the end of the chapter, is a summation of this belief. The poetic vision he lends to his experiences and deep meditation on things we take for granted in our indifferent stride, shakes up our mental lethargy and prods us to reflect intensely on such matters.

From the sphere of spirituality, we go into an investigation of the word "Bhaiya" — meaning older brother — a tag given to him by his elder sister! From there onto his take on 'name' with which he plays a word game, replacing 'n' with 'f' and then with 'g'. He muses that though many Indians are named after gods and goddesses, ruefully few imbibe the virtues of their namesakes — "Religion has left its profound mark in the psyche of Indians, but has failed to alter their behavioral pattern."

Namesake

Whispers the tale of your character,
color and its fragrance merge to call it/ a Rose.
A lot matters, / if you remember/ the name...

In the next chapter, Southern Affiliation he talks of his association with the southern city of Chennai (Madras), whose charms have bitten him affectionately. His affiliation is further enhanced by Mr. Atreya Sarma, to whom he devotes a whole paragraph and dedicates the poem "Clarity."

"Rains" is an allusion to situations that bewilder and hurt him; those thoughts, crowds, disciplines in which he tends to get totally drenched. These 'rains' have inspired poems from his hemorrhaging heart. His scientifically trained mind believes that love is "a strong cerebral affair." It is the brain that rules the heart he feels and yet he says love is "a wonderful experience that enables you to feel your loved inside of you." How beautiful is that!

"My Master and the Cover" is the most significant chapter. He talks about his initiation into Kriyayoga by his beloved master; about Spiritual awakening through the rising *Kundalini* — the Divine Feminine force — whereby an aspirant experiences a 'winy trance'. In the glow of his awakening he also tries to justify the cover design as substantiating Yoga in the light of literature, though there could be many different interpretations, as the designer refuses to explain his creation. But even as he exults in his Awakening he laments the moral degradation of the world and is grateful for his Master who helps him uncover the mysteries of life.

I

As identical as 'I'/ through the slice of my sigh.
Like the sky; where the stars shine bright and/ the Sun 'I'.

This book 'stirs' the reader to arouse his sleeping *Kundalini*.

Not charioted by Bacchus and his pards: Kiriti Sengupta's *My Glass of Wine*
Rumpa Das

Kiriti Sengupta's book, *My Glass of Wine* defies categorization! And it is not just because the book — a slender volume of some eighty-eight pages — is a matrix of personal recollections, philosophical musings, a mèlange of scattered images, memories and thoughts, but because in its open defiance to conform known generic categories, this David of a book challenges Goliaths of prose, poetry, poetic prose or prosaic poetry.

There have been a number of people like Dr Sengupta who are professionally not allied to literature. He may have lost his opportunity to study Masters in Community Dental Practice, but he did — like IAS officer Mamang Dai or former RAW Director and IPS officer Keki Daruwalla or orthopaedic surgeon Amitabh Mitra – listen to the bidding of his Muse. And that is why this simple, humble, hard-working medical practitioner –who once wasn't even aware of Tagore's masterpiece, *Sesher Kobita (The Final Verses)*, pampered his pen and poured his 'heartfelt words' that became *My Glass of Wine*. There have been quite a number of poets who are/were professionally engaged in apparently non-literary vocations, and though Dr Sengupta resists being tagged as an Indian English writer, it is a fact that more and more people from all walks of life are finding English and Indian English (Should we say Indish?) as an appropriate medium for articulating the pent-up poetry in their city-scarred souls. Dr Sengupta, no wonder, unburdens himself in his lines, serenely oblivious to the conventional dictates of form, terminology or genre! And why not? Why should a creator concern him/herself about the form, as long as the process of creation is cathartic? Why should a creative persona be bogged down by expectations to fit in? Why should the springs of poetry pause to ruminate which pre-charted course it should take? And so, *My Glass of Wine* intoxicates as it progresses through different sections — "As I Traversed," "My Glass Of Wine," "My Sister's *Bhaiya*," "Southern Affiliation," "Rains," "Clips," and "My Master and The Cover," until the beaded bubbles overflowing at the brim brushes past the readers' sensibilities and very covertly, announces its objective — why the nomenclature? Why the glass of wine?

However heady it might sound, Dr Sengupta's book is not about vineyards, wine, intoxication, or 'Bacchus and his pards' as Keats remarked in his celebrated "Ode to a Nightingale." Rather, in this book of poems, the first taste of wine one has is of the divine blood of the Sacrament, followed by the alcoholic beverages that are an intrinsic part of tantric rituals, and the last part deals with the Islamic ritual of oblation — the *Qurbani* which blends vignettes of sacrificial blood, impassioned chants, deafening shrieks, alcohol-induced hypnoses, orgies of power!

*It was not branded, but a homemade
Wine.
Intimately divine...
You and I
The Father and son
The legacy goes on.
Inevitable — impeccable,
Blood relation...*

The religious element associated with the wine effectively annihilates any prosaic or profane connotation, though poetry has, since time immemorial, been linked with wine and/or women. In Kiriti Sengupta's book, wine is divested of any irreverent associations and women too exist only in reverential roles - as his sweetheart (as he talks about fondly of his wife), mother (his mother being his initiator to the magic world of the English language), his sister or a woman-friend who was intent on getting him baptized. In the poems penned down by Sengupta, one comes across different faces of womanhood, all of them respectfully etched. The womb carries water — so do your eyes,

*Water builds the fetus
That becomes I . . .
It's a room for your eyes;
Under the name
'Rely.'*

The final section on "My Master and The Cover" is clearly the pièce de résistance in this volume of poems.

And it is here that Sengupta talks of the supreme among all woman-forces – the mother energy called *Kundalini* that, once awakened, ascends through *Sushumna Nadi* that is located between the *Ida* and the *Pingala* — a philosophical revelation that his master, Dr Ashoke Kumar Chatterjee initiated through the austere practice of Kriyayoga. Enunciated by Yogiraj Shyamacharan Lahiri, the doctrine of Kriyayoga reveals how 'the aspirant is able to taste the rich nectar wine that is said to be secreted from the cerebral region'. Sengupta juxtaposes this ardent belief that buoys up his existence with the cancer of moral corruption that threatens contemporary society at large – murders, rapes, betrayals and dishonesty in every aspect of life. In a question which this reviewer posed to him on the event of his book-launch, Sengupta on asked whether he believed that today's readers whose sensibilities are gradually being desiccated by the global threat of corruption can respond to his therapeutic spiritualism, confidently asserted that he believed that if he could rise, so could the teeming millions. In what reads like a stroke of celestial coincidence, Sengupta reveals how his cover-designer's illustration came to be an exact replica of his own abstract conception of spirituality that he aimed to represent, and like the poet himself, the designer too refused to elucidate much on his handiwork.

Keats once said famously, "If poetry comes not as naturally as the leaves to a tree it had better not come at all." For Kiriti, poetry comes naturally as does the prose pieces accompanying his poetic effusions. Interestingly, this is his third poetic foray, the earlier two being *The Unheard I* and *The Reciting Pens*. Here, in this book that combines memoir, autobiography, non-fictional prose and poetry, Kiriti's unheard 'I' is articulated; his pen starts reciting the music of his soul, the music the soul imbibes from his intimations with spirituality, with nature, with people, with the universe that he perceives. Kiriti Sengupta's book is a bricolage that reveals as much as it hides; like the poet, the reader too becomes a bricoleur who responds to the myriad hues of the creation in his unique way. The reader and the poet coalesce; the poet's intuition merges with the reader's perception, and *My Glass of Wine* has its desired effect.

As identical as 'I'
Through the slice of my sigh.
Like the sky;
Where the stars shine bright and
The Sun 'I'.

My Glass of Wine — A Trendsetting Ensemble

Seshu Chamarty

I ordered just two copies of this unique book because I went only by the title — what with my limitations on tippling. So the book remained uncorked in my cupboard for two weeks. Presto, I got myself freed from my other commitments today. Oh boy, I never knew when I finished the book! I raced through it which gave little resistance. Besides I felt no need to look up any single word. From the outside, the contents are unassuming like any strong wine. I also found the book a departmental store, sans the usual apparent labyrinths. I traversed effortlessly as though placed on a conveyer belt gliding seamlessly through the interface between prose, verse, and nonfiction laced with autobiography.

I recollected my journey to Darjeeling some years ago via Siliguri. Kiriti is connected to this place as per the book. While reading his book, I got an illusion that the author himself was sitting across from me in the train and reading out the text to me.

His narrative is both windy and sedate like I was on a rollercoaster of a train. Sometimes I was treated with some hardboiled home truths including life in India, and at other times interesting tidbits of his personal and intellectual life, throwing in a dash of professional dentistry and humor in between. He quoted some precious gems by great men eloquently and aptly. I did not open my mouth throughout 'his readings,' lest I would make him veer off the track.

By the way, I am used to seeing a verse embossed in the corner of a picture in Japanese Haiga poetry, and also verses juxtaposed with prose in Japanese Haibun. I saw traces of both those creative forms blended here in this book as if they are 'on the house,' without the author knowing that I am sure. I wish he should seriously imbibe those poetic forms too, in his future books. His autobiographical account is so unique that I can hardly see a parallel in any others.

When I completed my bout with this gem of a book, I checked my feet. They are yet steady but not with my mind; the author was still talking to me. I borrow here one of his 'clippings' among the vignettes, though not illustrative of his entire little book:

Vermillion

My earphone whispers, and
lips glued to the chewing gum.
My glasses moisten
as I find you eyesome.
Is this what they call love?

I wondered how a doctor could dare to go on a trip like this and succeed in impressing humble readers like me, as he did. The entire experience is like savoring the aroma (using his very similes) from the innocuous milk on the stove along with its pure cream being condensed, that is headier like vintage wine as shown on the cover page. Kiriti's spiritual and at the same time down-to-earth views including his opinion on what poetry ought to be (although he is averse to call himself a reformer) are badly needed in the present electronic age. Lay readers are feeling bored to read heavy prose and longwinded poems. Reading habits are radically refined to lap up colored images and word pictures as screened before their eyes.

His novelette is like 'instant coffee' in literature world, likely to be a trendsetter as an ensemble of lyrics, anecdotes, pictures, homilies, and last but not the least, life's philosophy in clinical yet poetic as well as light prose form. Further the book presents the author inside out — and we look at a true and transparent persona beside a good human being in his inimitable and delectable offbeat genre.

Reverse Out
Gopal Lahiri

Kiriti Sengupta's *The Reverse Tree* unfolds with intricate details and unexpected delights, and it reveals the disparate realities of life through seamless fusion. One will look in vain perhaps for something mystic or magical but Sengupta's dissection of the lifeline experiences, and the literary tone of his voice, set this book above his contemporary writers.

Sengupta is candid as always: "I believe when lives can be random, why would I possibly plan to order and smoothen the transitions? Let them remain as it is." In his foreword, Don Martin, the editor has remarked that he liked two things of Sengupta: "The first is how honest he (Sengupta) is," and the second thing "...he can make the cultural aspects of his work understandable to those who may not be so familiar with them."

There are six chapters in this book and they are imaginatively inventive to understand the meaning of life. Each chapter represents the working out of a single idea of randomness yet the question remains as Sengupta stated on a different context, "How does one get into another being so effortlessly?" Stories, sub-stories, subtle poems and backstories of biological clock, recipe for making *laccha parantha*, mimicry, long haired male poets and feminine metaphors (Kiriti admitted once: "men are my keys"), transgender woman and the embedded values in reversals abound though at the center of way of his writings is the spiritual essence. It's an amalgam of hues and textures, introducing a new dimension to the narrative that is vastly different from the traditional up and down staffs.

One of the ways, he's chosen to explore the issues through honest admission be it the skin color and racial overtone, or gay-sex and criminal offence, etc. Sometimes his characters are in crisis and chaos but fight back at the end.

"Living as a transgender is not an easy task, to say the least. I have seen Lara managing the role of a female that she was not bestowed with, but she was a free spirit and took up the challenges with full enthusiasm." (Crisis)

Sengupta's thoughts on dissecting humans are intriguing. In his creative world everything, even the steamy desires are joined and unified.

I have my own equation of love

my he throbs in fire

while my she is coy (Crisis)

There are wonderful sentences attempting to capture something that most conventional writings, with their usual plot and scene norms fail to do: the drift of thought, the snippets of undramatic life and the unheard music that compounds with the intensity that is lyrical and romantic yet distant and dissonant.

> *I know the shape of fish-lip*
> *gives hint of the water color deep*
>
> ...
>
> *my lips are thin*
> *no trace of color, but water*

There is a poem on "sleep" that provides an extraordinary view of events,

> *I see sleep*
> *sitting idle both side*
> *beneath my eyes*
>
> ...
>
> *but only two of us*
> *in the room for one* (Jetlag)

Sengupta writes personal anecdotes, pain and anguish in life and his clear eyed attention brings each topic into dizzying focus. Paying his tribute to his mother, Sengupta wrote, "If I am asked to pick a single teacher who has shaped me and my life, I will mention my mother." Writing personal and public with equal efficiency, his work contains a lot of useful and interesting information about the way the world wags these days. He makes his write all that easy yet his wit and analytical mind that create the immediacy.

More often than not, Sengupta allows us to have a private glimpse of his creative mind. His prose is a tale of our time, a powerful condemnation of inequality and animal instincts. Again as in the case of a few selected writers, he has a great gift for clarity; his prose is precise and heartfelt — achieving a timeless, polished quality, and his words especially in his poems heighten his emotions.

Talking about reversals, Don Martin observed, "May be it is more accurate to say that the reversal is more along the lines of things not always being what you might expect them." Sengupta has figured out *"The Geeta* is the most precious gift to our civilization that has been much endangered by the animal instincts of humans. Reversal of such animal instincts deserves austerity and it demands our strict adherence to the lessons as laid down in the chapters." He has introduced a new way of forcing the changes in life in reversals that are multivalent and varied and you can almost hear the resonance in the following poem,

the shoot is long and thick
smoother skin palpating beneath
no study of the plants, but of humans
the words of mouth
call upon true reversal
(Reversal … Reverse All)

Everything in Sengupta is connected; more than that, everything is infused, or always infusing. No other book in recent times includes and enacts so much, and we feel as we read that we are dealing in spiritual essence and distillation.

"*The Reverse Tree* is all about our understanding of the existence of mankind," Sengupta said. For all its richness it has a simple tale to tell: we are only ever a fraction of ourselves because most of what we are continuous under or alongside our consciousness, unseen, unknown, uncharted, and we need to reverse it out. Never tiresome, this book explores the heart of the issues and it is this that the arguments are riotously broad in its canvas and intimate in its portrayal of lives undone and forged anew. Sengupta never indulges in wrestling with grand themes.

There is no denying that *The Reverse Tree* has a beguiling mixture of lightness and weight, and most definitely it is a big step forward for the author to create a space for his readers and perhaps it is much more than that. It is a chronicle of the spiritual life that gets decanted unobtrusively in his work and has the appearance of effortlessness.

Fragmented Narratives in a Stream of Consciousness

Usha Kishore

It is difficult to place Kiriti Sengupta's novelette, *The Reverse Tree* in any one genre. It is a mélange of autobiography, non-conformism, magic realism and spirituality; it gets even more complex, when one of the thematic elements happens to be the transgender issue in India. Verse and prose are juxtaposed in this hybrid fiction that can be fittingly termed a monologue. The narrative moves from light hearted satire to sobriety, to counter narrative and philosophy. The issues of gender and transgender transcend the experimental format and venture into the realm of Indian socio-politics.

The reader is taken on a roller coaster ride of quick paced fragmented narratives in a stream of consciousness mode, meandering through a metafictional, monologic address to the reader, narrative gaps that leaves one gaping, creative writing exercises, the process of translation and a reflection on spirituality based on *The Bhagavad Gita*. Perhaps the best way to approach the book is to follow the writer, who takes you by hand on a journey through an Indian setting into the labyrinth of childhood, friendships, his medical practice, his reflections on the banyan tree (the reverse tree with aerial roots), the state of affairs with his transgender character Lara, his tenets on (trans) gender issues in India and a metaphorical closure of the journey, with philosophic reflections on *The Bhagavad Gita*.

The novelette opens with a poem that personifies "the reverse tree."

*my tree is stout,
well-developed
it refutes the gravitational pull
not always, you know...
my roots run
against the sap!*

This allegorical verse summarizes the book and its inclination of going against the grain. In the opening section entitled *Anti-Clock*, Sengupta addresses gender inequality by questioning male dominance in "family trees," especially when men cannot bear fruit. The rhetorical questions that address the reader in this section pose a serious challenge to Indian patriarchy. The writer opines: "Men are not physiologically enabled to bear the fruits of production, and thus they are the non-yielding entities."

A poignant and rather bold illustration of the plight of transgender individuals in contemporary India lies in the framed narrative of Lara's story. In India, gay sex is a punishable offence under Section 377 of the Indian Legislative Code; Sengupta remarks in a tongue in cheek fashion: "India being the spiritual kingdom of the world, is dangerously defying the scriptural implications, as gay sex has been banned by the Supreme Court of India." The author interrogates the Indian socio-cultural attitude towards LGBT individuals, which is defying the Vedic classification of *Purush, Stree* and *Trittiya Prakriti* (The Third Sex — attributed to LGBT individuals, according to authorial interpretation). Sengupta highlights the bias against homosexuals and transgender/transsexual individuals in India and wonders how such a law can possibly exist in the world's largest democracy. The author is convinced that his work would be termed by the literary fraternity as 'alternative poetry', as illustrated by the plucky and thought provoking erotic verse that introduces Lara's story:

you entered deep into me as did sleep
the moon shined bright
in your seminal light
for many nights ... for many nights

The creative light of the moon transforms into the creative energy of the novelist. In Indian Literature, the moon is seen as the comrade of lovers – the controversial connotation here is to lovers as in a homosexual relationship. The moon is also used here as a symbol of sexuality as it tends to affect the human moods in its waxing and waning forms.

The transgendered elements in Sengupta's translation of Sumita Nandy's *Ichemoti* in the book, *Desirous Water*, elicit layers of interpretations: the hermaphrodite entity that is part of all human beings, the *Ardhanarishwara* form of Shiva (Perhaps this is my alternative interpretation, befitting the alternative narrative within the novella.) or the Vedic "third sex" as interpreted by the writer on a metafictional note:

I've my own equation of love
my he throbs in fire
while my she is coy...
I worship the sun
powered by the rays
my she gives her all
as my he turns gay

The final section, "Reversal ... Reverse All" introduces the reader to the battlefield of Kurukshetra, where Krishna expounds the philosophy of battle and of life to Arjuna. Several verses of *The Gita* are quoted and translations provided, with references to various contexts. The most noteworthy factor here is the metafictional element in the role of a translator, who lets the soul of the original poet enter him: "An efficient translator constructs a faithful mirror that reflects the soul of the original literature." This idea is substantiated by a translation of verse II.22 from *The Gita*:

As a person puts on new garments while giving up the older ones, similarly the soul accepts new worldly bodies, quitting the old and useless ones. The novelette closes on a philosophic note, poetizing the surreal Reverse Tree to form a virtual circle within the novella:

numerous branches of the root
unite into two soft halves

some creases fine facing the sky
here the sun fails to light
the cloud fails to moisten
nature shelters the root
secures within an encapsulating tough skin
the shoot is long and thick
smoother skin palpating beneath.
no study of the plants, but of humans,
the words of mouth
call upon true reversal

The banyan tree symbolizes the human consciousness. The tree, considered to be the tree of life in Hindu scriptures, with its roots in the sky, branches on earth and leaves that are Vedic hymns, forms the quintessence of the book. As the author suggests *The Reverse Tree* is a metonym for our understanding of mankind. It is left to reader response as to how the reversal is interpreted- whether it is a metaphorical reversal of the human psyche or recognition of socio-cultural norms that are considered anti-establishment.

From "a non-poet writing poetry," *The Reverse Tree* has done well for itself on the poetic front. As a reviewer specializing in poetry, I find that the verses in this hybrid novella excel the prose, which could perhaps be adorned with more stylistic paraphernalia. In this journey through the book, you cannot but admire the panache of the man, who chooses to experiment with this kind of alternative narrative. His editor Don Martin rightly warns the readers in the foreword: "Waiting for a new Kiriti Sengupta book is always a tense time. I never really know what the next work will be, but I will say it is fun to anticipate what might come!" In his future works, would Sengupta venture further into this surrealist non-conformism?

A (Re)Versed World
Soumen Jana

How assured one feels when the exquisite cover page of the novelette — *The Reverse Tree* by Kiriti Sengupta — announces: "trespassers won't be prosecuted.../this is all about you & me!" With such an open-to-all invitation, I did not dare rebuff the air of camaraderie the words promise; I rather set out, murmuring like that Eliotian figure — "Let us go then, you and I." But the casual in me had soon been accosted and warned both by the author and the editor of the book. The author sounds a caution — "Be a bit cautious, dear reader, you won't find a smooth transition from one chapter to another." Luckily, I got alarmed timely. And I must say that while approaching the book, one must not make the mistake of judging it by its size.

Sengupta's book is surely not a voluminous one, just sixty-two pages long. It is comprised of six seemingly unrelated brief chapters (the largest one spans just ten pages or so!): "Anti-Clock," "In Other's Shoes," "Long ... A Metaphor," "Crisis," "Jet Lag," and "Reversal ... Reverse All." All these could have gone against the noble ventures of its author. But the strength of the book lies in what could have been for many blocks of weakness or shortcoming: its uncanny precision, its unmistakable casualness in tone intermixed with occasional gravity of the subject matter, and most importantly its immaculate simplicity of narration coupled with enticing poeticism in its language. What is contained inside this slimmest structure is a mine of dynamite: all it needs is a spark in the form of concentration and a bit meditation and mediation, and what it gives, besides many things, is a spark in the form of self-realization.

However, while talking about the idiosyncratic nature of treatment its author often does to his subjects in his other works (that are mostly variegated in color and eclectic in subject-matter), Don Martin, the editor of the book, rightly sounds a cautionary note to those who expect an easy flow of thought or a linear story crystallized on the pages between the two covers or are much concerned with a fixed destination or a clear-cut moralizing at the end. Its readers must be cognizant of the fact that, while the book does not set forward a 'story,' it certainly offers 'a take' which is unfortunately not 'the conclusion' a casual reader wants to arrive at effortlessly. The pages are strewn with potent 'signifiers.' What the readers need to do is to connect the dots the way they are conditioned. Whatever their conclusions or whichever way they are reached, one cannot escape the psychedelic experience its reading provides. Of absence of any overt connection among the chapters, the author himself in Introduction says, "My life has never sailed smoothly.... I believe, when lives can be random, why would I possibly plan to order and smoothen the transitions? Let them remain as it is..." We get an explanation and a foreboding that once in, the reader will simply be taken away along the stream of consciousness — the consciousness of the author and the consciousness of the reader intersecting at points, not at will but by common sharing — only to be washed ashore on the banks of the ultimate impartial indivisible Consciousness or Soul. But it must be mentioned that it's not sermonic. I will take up this issue later on.

Now of its one connecting link, the editor of the book mentions, "But keep in mind, as you read *The Reverse Tree*, that not everything is what it may appear to be!" (This section of the book is named interestingly enough — "Leading Along The Path To Understanding!"). The theme of 'reversal' in its multidimensionality seems to link the different episodes. Before one reaches its first chapter, "Anti-Clock" (the briefest of them, just a page-length!), one lands onto apparently a wayward poem:

my tree is stout,
well-developed
it refutes gravitational pull

not always, you know...

my roots run
against the sap!

The image of a 'stout' tree, refuting 'gravitational pull' with roots running 'against the sap' does not scintillate any bleakness or pessimism, it is the image of one (may well be a self-portrait) who loves treading the untraded path, one who has the guts to be centrifugal, to be 'unconventional' in attitude and treatment. It also hints the image of a 'reversed' tree which is explained in the concluding section of the book. However, it strikes the note of 'alterity' and the reader is made prepared to deal with its inherent unconventionality. This note, along with the image of tree, is carried forward to the first chapter. "Anti-Clock" turns upside-down the male-image and the superiority attached by making some significant observations:

> Men are not physiologically enabled to bear the fruits of production, and thus they are the non-yielding entities. Men are often referred to as trees, especially in familial setups, but none has specified yet if they are the male trees, which don't bear the fruits of love ... Men are expected to be masculine, hence non-flowery. They are seedy, but are not eligible to carry the fruits ... it is the ladies who turn out to provide better shade than the men. (Page 1)

The in-vogue power-equation is challenged.

The next chapter — "In Other's Shoes" is a tale of mimicry. The author narrates in humorous tone how he met, after a long gap, his friend Shouvanik Dey (who is good in getting into the soul of the person or thing he mimics, we are told), and how exquisitely, in a funny and lively way, he presents a complete replica of a Youtube session (with all its buffering and peculiarities) to teach the author how to prepare *laccha parantha*. Now behind the veneer of this funny act lies a gesture towards complete understanding which can only be achieved through suspension of the 'self' and by assuming the 'selfness' of the 'other.' Thus, a collapse of inkless barriers nurtured by ego shall bring wisdom and understanding, and can effortlessly solve a lot of problems the world suffers for just matters of miscommunication, for not being able to get into another being, for not being able to see the other's view.

The third chapter — "Long...A Metaphor" speaks of the taken for granted status of the long-haired poets (as if keeping long hair guarantees creative brilliance and extraordinariness!) and exhorts the readers to investigate if there is really any serious connection between long hair and poetry or art. What is interesting about male artists sporting a feminine metaphor (keeping long hair is associated with women generally) is the implicated subversion of prefixed gender roles. The metaphors need serious attention (may be re-working or re-adjusting). However, the long poem beautifully records the encounter of the author with a long-haired poet who speaks of him dismissively just for he has long hair!

The next chapter — Crisis" is the most polemic since here the author takes up the issue of sex and gender roles, of bisexuality, homosexuality, transgenders and sexual preference, of his professional life as a doctor, and of his meeting with Lara, a transgender who finally decided to be a women and her pathetic but inspiring tale. An inquisitive Sengupta, in relation to a mix of the both sexes — male and female — in the poetic voice in Sumita Nandi's "Ichemoti," quips — "Is this what we refer to as a third sex or gender?" Perhaps. Perhaps not. But obviously in such a mix of sexes (or gendered sensibilities), there is a possibility of apotheosizing the ideal male-female union, as in the image of *Ardhanarishwar* (in Hindu belief) or of aestheticizing the whole experience. For instance, take a few lines from the beautiful poem Sengupta wrote as he read Sumita Nandi's "Desirous Water" (translation of "Ichemoti"):

> *I've my own equation of love*
> *my he throbs in fire*
> *while my she is coy* …(page 11)

This is, even the author will agree, aesthetically the most satisfying experience and so much apolitical too. But what's about the total LGBT clan and their experiences? Sengupta's concern here is their real rights and treatment they should enjoy purely as a human being first since he knows "…living as a transgender is not an easy task…" And since the Indian Vedic literature speaks of three distinct sex-categories (*Purush* or male, *Stree* or female, and *Tritiya Prakiti* or the third sex) and since it's the world's largest democracy, Sengupta wonders how can India and its unruly laws become so insensible to this *Tritiya Prakriti*? The Supreme Court of India by banning gay sex under section 377 of the Indian Legislative Code as a punishable offence not only defies the 'scriptural implications' (Page 13) but also violates human rights. This is where a serious reversal of attitude is needed. As he says—

> I think, none is black or white when it comes to representing sexual orientation or biasness. We all are biased … colors mark racial discrimination. (Page 13)

And "sexual acts between two consenting adults (irrespective of their genders) can never be termed crime" (Page 14). The narrative concerning the life of Lara not only showcases a blistered face of democracy but also sets forth a possibility as Lara is able to live life on her own terms. This is again a reversal in attitude the transgenders need to inculcate.

In the fifth chapter, "Jet Lag," the author offers us an amazing poem on sleeplessness and speaks of his writing spree that 'made a non-poet write poetry'. But more than that what this chapters contributes to the whole scheme of the novelette is the reversal of our idea about 'jet lag'. He writes:

> Although jet-lag affects our sleep pattern, it is not necessarily associated with the differences in time zones. Jet-lag is also induced by the differences in attitude of the people who facilitate the transit from one country to another. (Page 23)

It's the final chapter — "Reversal ... Reverse All" that first formally introduces its reader with the features of 'the reverse tree', the description of which we find in the *Srimad Bhagavad Geeta*, the last scripture of *Santana Dharma*: it is a tree "that stands upside down ... that grows in reverse order"(Page 25). Sengupta quotes some of his favorite verses and tries to interpret them vis-a-vis his society and literature. Thus here we are introduced to a plethora of subjects – from the recent Israel-Gaza conflict to what religion is, what scriptures actually stand for, how a proper translation should be, what the soul is, who is true master and in this context his mother's indelible influence on his being. But what ultimately is to mesmerize the reader is its aligning of the image of 'the reverse tree' with that of a human being—

> Humans are the only such trees that have their roots (brain) up and the branches (limbs) down. (Page 34)

The reader is sure to be overwhelmed with this grave realization, knowing what exactly the reverse tree is.

It must be clarified, on the basis of whatever I have understood, that 'reversal' here is not Bakhtinian carnival; it certainly does unsettle the power-equations of male-female, but it's more than that. It is reversal in/of attitude, in/of the ways we look at things. It is not going backward but moving forward to self-actualization. Sengupta wisely remarks –

> …reversal demands practice of the principles that lead us towards truth or realization. Human-birth is graced as one understands the challenges of life and implements wisdom to stand up to them. *The Reverse Tree* is all about our understanding of the existence of mankind…

> *I'm no linguist…*
> *I know*
> *air and age are linked*
> *since eternity…*
>
> *and the wounds surface again*
> *in all directions…*
> *Sporting the guise of youth…* (Page 36)

Needless to say the book is a glimpse into the 'personal' of its author and the author never seems to shy away from unfurling his private self. But for that I think he should not be called unabashed. Instead, it does the much-needed service of adding authenticity. But then it must not be termed as purely autobiographical. Just as it is not out and out religious. To some extent it's spiritual but more than that it's a translation of thoughts intended to arouse kindred thoughts to effect a true reversal(s). Of its poetic trait, it will not be an overstatement to say that, it is a book of poems often punctuated with prose passages that again sometimes border on being poetic. Moreover, the illustrations between the covers and cover-design do almost half the work in forming an idea of the book.

Man in the Botanical Garden: The Fallen, the Forbidden, the Golden, the Heaven-Going Tree versus the Tree Turned Upside Down

Bishnupada Ray

In the beginning man was hermaphrodite, a man-tree carrying both fruit and seed in the wake of it. But in a masterstroke of evolution the tree fell, its fruits fell off and the seeds spilled. From the seeds came two separate entities, sex-wise, male and female, and gender-wise, man and woman. They were so different in body and mind that without looking at each other, soon went in opposite ways in desperation. But both soon suffered the desperation of a yearning to seek out the other. This was love. Out of this desperation they sought fulfillment in the other. But out of the same desperation they were in perpetual flight, perpetually withdrawing from each other, in perpetual disagreement. Man never experienced such an aggravated sense of Eros and Thanatos as in this twin manifestation.

Or in the Garden of Eden man was alone and lonely, so God created woman from man's rib bone to be his partner; a partner in life and a partner in death; a partner in his rise and in his fall; a partner in his glory and in his shame. It was a divine bond beyond and at the same time around the Forbidden Tree of consciousness, the consciousness of good and evil. When the forbidden tree bore fruit it was woman who ate the fruit first, so she also became capable of bearing fruit and she gave the seeds to man to eat.

Or in the sacred grove of Nemi in ancient Rome there had been a golden tree. Anybody breaking a branch of this tree would have become a priest-king. So the reigning priest-king had to defend the tree from any challenger aspiring to break a branch, by remaining on guard all the time and by maintaining a round the clock vigil. The power struggle or the blood conflict eventually got transformed into a psychological conflict of ego and around the golden tree man and woman were seen lurking in ambush.

Or in the Old Norse mythology there is yggdrasil or the heaven-going tree that acts like a stairway to heaven. Is this tree a woman, capable of redeeming the fallen man?

Perhaps all these trees get connected in the surreal tree that Kiriti Sengupta presents us in his latest book *The Reverse Tree* which he describes as a crisis-management autobiographical philosophy. The man-woman problematic leads him to reverse the fallen man-tree towards the original androgynous *ardhanariswar* position but he turns it upside down keeping in view the contemporary gender issues to show his reverse tree caught in a time warp. He seems to probe into this seemingly unending sex-dilemma which is all too human to humanly decipher by changing the metaphor in each chapter. The hypothetical, the comic, the poetic, the physical, the voyeuristic and the spiritual sides of the same quest are recorded with a human cry for compassion and a human will for divine grace. One can understand his anxiety in the question, "would you still like to consider men as trees?" I once heard an educated lady saying that man was a tree, the more stout the tree was the more bliss your golden deer (read 'woman') would get by rubbing onto it. Here is his prologue:

>*my tree is stout,*
>*well-developed*
>*it refutes the gravitational pull*

>*not always, you know…*

>*my roots run*
>*against the sap!*

However an uncertainty and a question of 'life in death' and 'death in life' is indicated as well in the prologue. A non-stout tree is unsuitable for the golden deer of magical forests and a man is helpless except he turns into a poet dreaming and churning out 'poetree' in his incapacity. Is a poet masculine or masculine enough to have a smooth sailing? I have doubts. The poet is a crucifix standing in wilderness of life awaiting the arrival of meanings to purify his soul so that he remains a spiritual martyr. Then why this concern to keep the soul immaculate in the process of its translation through life? The body must die for its sins. Similarly the soul must live by its own virtue. The body is experienced but it is transcended to keep the soul intact. Is not the body as divine as the 'sap' through which your 'roots' penetrate? Then why only the body is transgressed and violated just because you have a false sense of identity? Then what is an identity? There is nothing truer than your true being even when that gets deluded by the golden deer of 'becoming'. Then why fear the false prophets, the 'editors' of falsity and artificiality? The body is immediate and contingent, the soul distant but urgent. Body is pain, blood, sweat, tears, guts (Clara); the soul is an untouchable (the narrator). The poet is a body, a failed body, a spurned and violated body, a body reserved for post mortem (like the inspection of Clara's suture) but it is a body that redeems others, enables others to have a soul. The poet is the totemic 'I' without which life is meaningless.

I am sure that *The Reverse Tree* will mark a turning point in the writer's life and art as evident from his serious and engaging questions about the areas of life not so well-lighted or clearly defined. Hope he will continue his philosophical quest towards enlightenment.

The Reverse Tree — a review
Eileen Register

India has always been a mystery to me. I've often thought it would be an interesting place to visit. When I read Kiriti Sengupta's book, *My Glass of Wine,* I began to discover many things about that fascinating place. With the author's latest book, *The Reverse Tree*, my education continued, but not only that. Sengupta's unique style and his openness about himself, his life, and his views on various subjects have increased my fascination with his country, but more so with the mindset of the author. *The Reverse Tree,* which has been called a novelette, is more of a poetic exploration of the author as a writer and as a man.

The Reverse Tree is not a thick book. In fact, it contains just six brief chapters, but what Sengupta has to say is far more interesting and informative than the reader may find in much thicker books. He touches on such things as the differences between women and men, mimicry and the difficulty of stepping into another person's shoes, and the author's fascination with long-haired poets. The longest and perhaps the most controversial chapter explores the almost taboo subject (at least in India) of "the third sex." Sengupta rounds off his far-flung subject matter with an informative discussion of The Gaeta, and finally, an explanation of the reverse tree – both as a real tree and as a metaphor. Throughout the book, the author presents poems, some that make perfect sense to this American reviewer and some that take thought on the part of the reader to discern their meaning and how they relate to the subjects about which they expound.

Taken as a whole, Sengupta's *The Reverse Tree* may seem like a "stream of consciousness" piece in that there are no transitions linking the six chapters. The author explains his reason for this in his introduction:

> I believe, when lives can be random, why would I possibly plan to order and smoothen the transitions? Let them remain as it is ... I will let you probe the real author!

Indeed, the reader is given random views into the heart and mind of Kiriti Sengupta.

From a woman's perspective, the author's views on men and women may seem somewhat sexist, but taken in context with Sengupta's Indian upbringing and culture, they begin to make sense. He compares men to trees:

> If I ask you, what comes to your mind immediately as you think of a tree? I'm sure that your reply will include all or any of the following: a) flowers, b) fruits, c) green, or d) shade. Men are expected to be masculine, hence

non-flowery. They are seedy, but are not eligible to carry the fruits.

Thus men are participants in the production of the "fruits" but only by virtue of their seed. In his own way, Sengupta is glorifying the woman's important role as the bearer of the fruit. On the other hand, he points out the difference in the aging processes of men and women: "The signs of aging surface earlier in ladies, and men are ever-green." In his opinion, this may be men's only "saving grace" as women

> have proved their mettle as adequate servers in their families. With service evolves dependence, and honestly, it is the ladies who turn out to provide better shade than the men.

While women may be in a position of dependency, they are the comforters and caretakers of the family.

While pondering the author's statements regarding women's dependent role as the wife and mother in the family structure, I began to wonder how accurate Sengupta's suppositions are. One way of finding out was to compare the divorce rate of India with that of the United States. To my surprise, India has the lowest divorce rate in the world at 1.1% compared to at least 50% in the U.S., according to the website I viewed: (http://www.divorcepad.com/rate/divorce-rate-in-india.html). The article went on to say that the divorce rate is climbing in India:

> Whether it is the metros or the semi-urban areas, whether it is the upper class or the middle class, or any state or city in the country, the divorce problem persists and the divorce rates are only increasing with time.

The article gives as one of the reasons for the rising divorce rate:
> Women are now at par with men in financial terms and do not feel the need to depend on their husbands for their financial needs. Men are also good with their domestic responsibilities and do not need to depend on women for the same. These changing gender roles [have] also impacted the divorce rates in India.

Therefore, it seems to me that Sengupta's views about the roles of men and women in his culture may be becoming outdated as the roles of men and women in his country change. Perhaps this role reversal is part of the theme of *The Reverse Tree*. In the closing chapter of the book, the author points out that,
> Reversal happens indeed! It is not like the anti-aging crème that you may find in the beauty-salons, but reversal demands practice of the principles that lead us towards truth or realization. Human-birth is graced as one understands the challenges of life and implements wisdom to stand up to them.

"In Others' Shoes," Chapter 2 in Sengupta's book, relates a story about being visited by a friend, Shouvanik. When he offered to cook a meal for the friend, a discussion ensued in which his friend questioned why Sengupta used a recipe book to learn the recipe rather than going to an online source – specifically YouTube. When the internet refused to come online, Shouvanik proceeded to mimic the video he had viewed, bringing Sengupta much laughter in the process. Sengupta finishes the chapter with a question: "How does one get into another being so effortlessly?" The author wonders how his male friend was able to imitate a female so perfectly, and this question is explored again later in the book.

Chapter 3, "Long ... A Metaphor" is about long hair, especially long hair on some poets. The poem at the end of the chapter describes Sengupta's encounter with a "long-haired poet" and asks the readers to decide whether the poem is simply about hair or represents something more. Again, we see a side of the author that opens us to more understanding of his thoughts and views.

It is in Chapter 4, "Crisis," which is the longest chapter in the book, that Sengupta discusses the three sexes. Here he explains how the third sex is treated in his native country of India:

> In our ancient *Vedic* literature sex is clearly divided into three distinct categories, *Purush* or male, *Stree* or female, and *Tritiya Prakriti* or the third sex. Gay men, lesbians, transgenders and transsexuals are considered among the third sex.

He goes on to state:

> Under section 377 of the Indian Legislative Code gay sex is a punishable offence that may

extend up to life imprisonment. I wonder how such a law can possibly exist in the world's largest democracy! Now another question is if India is truly a democratic country. However, I strongly believe sexual acts between two consenting adults (irrespective of their genders) can never be termed crime. [Page 15]

Thus it is clear that Sengupta fails to understand how the "spiritual kingdom of the world," India, could have laws making the third sex's private, personal activities illegal.

The first poem in this chapter ends with the statement that *"my she gives her all as my he turns gay."* Although Sengupta does not claim at any point to be other than heterosexual, the reader may wonder whether this is true as he or she reads this entire chapter, which includes another poem and a story about the time the author met and medically helped a transsexual, becoming friends with her in the process. He states that India has alternative literature as well as alternative lifestyles and that he will not be insulted if his writings are considered to fit the alternative genre. He is a proponent of freedom to choose one's sexual orientation and to live as one sees fit; let the reader surmise what he or she will regarding what this chapter says about the author.

In "Jetlag," the fifth chapter of *The Reverse Tree*, the author jumps to an entirely new subject that embraces his recent insomnia and his nephew's experience traveling from the United States to India. First, he personifies "Sleep" as an entity occupying "the room for one." Many readers who have experienced the inability to find sleep will easily understand and identify with this poem which, in my opinion, is perhaps the best poem in the book.

Later in the chapter, Sengupta tells of his nephew's problems with jetlag when traveling from his new country of the United States to his homeland, India. He states:

> Although jet-lag affects our sleep pattern, it is not necessarily associated with the differences in time zones. Jet-lag is also induced by the differences in attitude of the people who facilitate the transit from one country to another. [Page 24]

The second poem in this chapter explains what he means, blaming a lot of what travelers feel after an international flight forward or backward in time due to time zones on how individual passengers are treated by immigration officers according to the color of the passenger's skin. I have never flown internationally, so I can't really relate to the actual physical manifestations of jetlag, but I can certainly understand what the author is expressing here. Racism exists all over the world. Discrimination isn't exclusive to one's skin color, though, as my sister and her husband, who have an Arab last name, face close scrutiny when traveling. They are both American citizens, but her husband originates from Jordon, and it is because of their last name that they have a more difficult time traveling outside the United States, and in deed, within the U.S. as well.

After reading the first five chapters of Kiriti Sengupta's book, in the final chapter, "Reversal ... Reverse All," the reader is finally told what is meant by "the reverse tree." The author states:
> *The Geeta* is the most precious gift to our civilization that has been much endangered by the animal-instincts of humans. Reversal of such animal instincts deserves austerity, and it demands our strict adherence to the lessons as laid down in the chapters.

After sharing his poem about the "Reverse Tree," Sengupta presents several verses from *The Geeta* and relates them to how various aspects of life reverse themselves. He discusses his work as a translator as well, explaining a particular verse in this way: A soul is an indivisible entity as *The Geeta* urges:
> *nainam chindanti sastrani nainam dahati pawakah na caiman kledyan tyapo na shosyati marutah*
>
> [*The soul can never be cut into pieces by any weapon, nor can it be burned by fire, nor moistened by water, nor withered by the wind.*] [Chapter II, verse 23]

He relates this verse to the work of translation:
> An efficient translator constructs a faithful mirror that reflects the soul of the original literature. The more the surface area of reflecting body, the better is the image formed.

Since the soul is indivisible, what a translator must seek to do is reflect the soul of the writer he translates to the best of his ability, recognizing that the full picture of

181

what the writer is saying may not totally translated from one language to another – in Sengupta's case, from Bengali to English. Although the author has stated in another area of his writings that he feels as though he has opened himself and allowed the soul of the writer he translates to enter him, he clarifies that statement with his application of this verse of *The Geeta* to the translation work. He follows this explanation with a poem in which he explains what he means when he uses the word "soul" – an interesting and insightful poetic view that attempts to enlighten the reader regarding the author's defining of that word.

Sengupta translates and explains several more verses of *The Geeta*, and after one of the verses, he discusses the teachers he has had during his lifetime. This brings him to a discussion of his own mother, who is a teacher, and to share a poem he wrote for her one Mother's Day. In it, he tells of a time when he was ill and his mother comforted him after a nightmare disturbed his sleep – another window into the life of the author.

Finally, Sengupta quotes and translates a verse from *The Geeta* that talks about the Banyan tree, a tree that grows with its roots upward and its branches and leaves downward. It is here from which he extrapolates his concept of reversal. I will leave this portion of the verses and the author's explanations unquoted, letting the reader discover on his or her own how the author explains this concept. I close this lengthy review with but one more quote:

The Reverse Tree is all about our understanding of the existence of mankind...

I'm no linguist

I know air and age are linked since eternity

*and the wounds surface again
in all directions…
sporting the guise of youth*

Healing Waters Floating Lamps — Lanterns, Fireflies, and Will-o'-the-Wisps

Vibha Malhotra

Kiriti Sengupta's book *Healing Waters Floating Lamps* is a cohesive collection of multi-layered, multi-directional poetry centered on various aspects of spirituality, both personal and universal. Don Martin, the editor of the book, says in his foreword, "There are some multi-layered meanings here, sometimes clothed in paradox and irony, and it can take some time and considered thought to find them." It is in the context of these words that the book is best explored, for on the surface the poems appear deceptively simple.

In some poems, spirituality runs deep, while in others it also runs on the surface. "In Dusty Feet" seems to be about following a master. It seems to be about Faith. Until you give it another read. Then emerge the questions of who you put your faith in, about the impact that has on you, about how God stays elusive if you try to look for divinity within the limits of our human existence. And, thus, *"God remains thumb-sized with dusty feet."*

Images that remain inaccessible to us despite being ubiquitous are brought to life in poems such as "Color Code" and "Clarity," but perhaps the most evocative imagery emerges in the poem "Eyes of a Yogi."

> *A mother bird sits on her eggs ... quiet...*
> *Her eyes appear distantly connected to the world*
>
> *Hey! Look at them*
> *Tiny wings*
>
> *The mother changes to sky*

Such poems make you wonder why we fail to notice beauty in the world around us when each little moment, each ephemeral sight, every tiny creature is capable of such deep spiritual connection with the world. With this realization, the world seems to turn resplendent as if some dark curtain has been lifted somewhere.

In his review of the book, eminent scholar Dr Ananya S Guha says, "But the subversive elements dominate the poems- this well ordered reality should be transcended into the metaphysics of life. It is a Meta world we live in. The poems reveal this intensity of grappling with prescient but not foreboding truths. Always there is light, not darkness." The book does tread through forsaken ruins with as much grace as it meanders through lush, green pastures. Spirituality is constant, omnipresent. It exists as serenely on the Ghats of Ganga in Varanasi as it does in a morgue. It is present in birth as much as in death. "Mellifluous Cry" exists somewhere in that realm – in between two stark realities:

The labor room was busy as usual
Especially the midwife
She was visibly unhappy with the silence of the newborn
Much worried at it, she patted the back of the baby

The midwife screamed in utter frustration
"Hey! Cry out."

It evokes a sense of losing an important part of yourself, the unbearable pain of someone precious fast moving out of your reach. It brings you face to face with your helplessness against death, and worse still, against the death of someone precious to you. But all is not lost yet. There is still hope. And that is where the poem leaves you – precariously balanced between life and death, suspended between hope and hopelessness.

But relief is close at hand and the poet does allow you some cozy, nostalgic moments at home, a peak into his past, and into yours too. "Clarity" dwells on the poet's memories of his childhood, his mother's diligence as she prepares Ghee. The process in essence is similar to the gradual purification of the soul, and the product in both cases is "pious" and "incorrigible."

Love, so intricately interwoven with spirituality, manifests itself in various forms across different poems – in togetherness, in loneliness, in yearning, in Sufi meditations. "Celluloid" captures the essence of transcendental love, where love survives even when one partner has declared that he or she is "Signing off for today."

Spirituality flows like ebb and flow of the tide through these short, staccato verses, like water in the womb, in eyes, in rivers, and in oceans. You find transcendence in unlikely places such as in the eyes of a mother bird and in a fish tank, and questions in places where you expect answers, such as in the yearnings of aged parents, in a river that bears Gods, in birth, in love, and in worship. And in this sense the lyrical title "Healing Waters Floating Lamps" mimics the overarching spiritual philosophy of the book, which is fluid like water and the verses that are like fireflies, each illuminating a separate, unique patch of darkness for a fraction of a second. This is not a book that can be read in a hurry or with a wandering, preoccupied mind. Pick it up when you are ready to commit some time to it. Because even after several readings, the book may leave you feeling restless, as if there is something crucial you have still missed in these verses, something that may make all the difference to your interpretation of the poems. But tread carefully, for these are treacherous grounds, and make sure what you are assuming is a lantern doesn't turn out to be a will-o'-the-wisp.

Journey with the Self
Sharmila Ray

Going through *Healing Waters Floating Lamps*, a selection of poems by Kiriti Sengupta made me remember few lines of Tocqueville (1835):

> "In democracies it is by no means the case that all who cultivate literature have received a literary education, and most of those who have some belles-lettres are engaged in professions that only allow them to taste occasionally and by stealth the pleasures of the mind. Accustomed to the struggle, the crosses, and the monotony of practical life, poets require strong and rapid emotions, startling passages, truths or errors brilliant enough to rouse them up and to plunge them at once, as if by violence, into the midst of the subject."

Why have I entertained these sentences is because the poet is a doctor by profession and going through his poems there is a feeling of well balanced liberation from the clutches of the laws of poetry. What emerges are encounters with the self, prodding the self to respond and contemplate.

This sleek volume with small poems are double-layered. First there is the observation with the five senses, the reality, we are comfortable with and then a second reading leads to another reality beyond words and sounds, smell and touch, where the 'I' withers to be at one with all.

The first poem in the volume "Beyond The Eyes" (mark the title) prepares the reader for other words, other lines on next pages of the book. It prepares us for an unknown universe, a space of different representations where the smell of infinity lingers.

I reach the sky
While I draw a circle in the water
Looking at the image
I take a dip

These lines invite the reader to take a dip in the water to create a world of their own. Water flows and so each pattern is replaced by another circle or oblong. In fact, transient. So is our material world.

As the poems progress the feeling of awareness snowballs into an all pervasive consciousness, an inner knowledge, attaining harmony with the outer world. Kiriti pushes us, prods us in each of his poems to listen, observe and be attentive to ourselves. The poet believes in living here and now in enjoying the world that encircles us and participating in the experience of the present. This is very much reflected in his poem titled "Celluloid."

...I was hesitant, you know,
I never said goodbye
Signs are private, and I keep my eyes open.
Round the clock.

As the collection winds its way down the path of aloneness, a journey with the self, a certain certitude emerge – like putting faith in ordinary things and not accepting old mental program and rejecting external manipulation.

...The word "denser" does not
Necessarily mean thicker... ("Secure A River")

Also in "Color Code":

They said you were black
They knew they were white
...
And I said
This has been the Nelson Mandela *patch.*

The poems in *Healing Waters Floating Lamps* are to be read slowly, to ponder and think. Take for instance the poem on Varanasi. The title is the key. Here the poet does not name the poem Evening in Varanasi. He writes "Evening Varanasi". As if Varanasi is a being, a symbol of spirituality. The mystic soul of India. Its body the meditating ground for those in search of oneness.

Have you seen the floating lamps in the river?
Water here is not the fire-extinguisher, but
The flames ascend through water
Prayers reach the meditating Lord

Both Bhagirath and Prometheus bought down river Ganga and Fire, respectively, from the heavens to bless mankind. So they are both images of life and all that is divine in the human. They are life-givers and mind-openers. The floating lamps are a reminder of this ephemeral world, which is floating and changing. Only mindfulness is real and that opens the door of super consciousness or God (*Prayers reach the meditating Lord*).

Again the poet very subtly plays with the theme of eternity in his poem "Memorandum Of Understanding". Age is a human perception and we cannot bottle air in ancient and medieval, modern and post-modern bottles.

...I know
Air and age are linked
Since eternity...

Kiriti's poems are a montage of responses to the everyday philosophy that runs subterranean in the orient. These experiences are common to all men. But the poet remembers them and give them form through words without frills. The poems are short and deeply suggestive, unlocking hidden areas of the self and not simply illustrating an object or an event. What is interesting that there are many ways of reading his poems. They are not restricted. They are like one long abstract painting, inviting the readers to come up with their own meaning, thereby making them participate in the poem. So as readers they are also writing. Perhaps, after reading Kiriti's poetry the reader would turn to love and compassion in these days of online shopping, virtual friends and emotions in the shapes of *smilies*.

Direct References to Life
Ananya S Guha

Kiriti Sengupta's poems are at once lonely, spiritual and a mystique of the open wide world punctuated with existential questions, In *Healing Waters Floating Lamps* the poet holds constant dialogue between what is signified — call it God, a moral question or retribution, or even a pantheistic credo. The persistent reference to water, the sea and the ethereal connote a world that is sacrosanct, such as the invocation of a holy city, or a Tagorean utterance of God and a hushed mystical world.

Throughout the poems there is a defiance of the ordinary as the poems catapult into an emblazoned extraordinary world. Yet the poems are not reductionist, they are structures embedded in a philosophy of humanity which is God-centered. The cultural stance that the poet takes is culled from everyday situations such as the apparent ordinariness of a fish depicting a cultural symbol.

The Tagorean impulse dominates some of the poems:

"*Have you seen the floating lamps in the river?*"
("Evening Varanasi")

Or "*My Master enjoys the stage*" ... ("Unravel")

While "Eyes Of A Yogi" ends with a crescendo "*The mother changes to sky.*"

These poems are not arid intellectualism. They are poetry of the heart, the spirit. Yet they are complex interfaces of existence. They are not subject to one interpretation. Such interpretative dimension imbue these with fine, subtle qualities.

Throughout the poems there are reverberations of the infinite pinned down by a finite well-ordered reality. But the subversive elements dominate the poems- this well ordered reality should be transcended into the metaphysics of life. It is a Meta world we live in. The poems reveal this intensity of grappling with prescient but not foreboding truths. Always there is light, not darkness:

"*I reach the sky
While I draw a circle in the water
Looking at the image
I take a dip*" ("Beyond The Eyes")

The poems militate against arid intellectualism. They open out the citadels of love, they are not susceptible to one interpretation, they are rather interpretative and multi-layered. They are irreducible statements not of the cerebral, but that of the spirit. This breaks new grounds in Indian English poetry.

The power of Sengupta's poetry lies within, not without. The images are retained inwardly and inner senses cry out for something, somewhere:

"I have seen my mother
Preparing Ghee out of milk-
She never used butter
To clarify it further..." (Clarity)

"Clarity" here assumes an ambiguous connotation. Do we have it in what we say and do? Sengupta's poems rest continuously in such clever word making and imagery. Let us look at the images in his poems: eyes, water, tears, river, yogi are some of them. The sacred city of Varanasi is another one. The poet is subsumed by a quest for the ordinary transformed into extraordinary metabolic desires. This gives to his poetry a pugnacity, barring any raucousness. The voice is always quiet, meditative, it is never sentimental or maudlin. If there is a cry for God, then it is an act of surrender. In fact surrender is one of the dominant themes of these poems. But it precludes any kind of overt religiosity. Sengupta's poems are no ontology, they are direct references to life, the rustic world and sometimes to relationships. They may be direct statements, but their innards are complex and philosophical. They maybe short poems, but they "say" much more than they state. A lot of Indian poetry in English today is pretentiously cerebral and exercises in word play which has become a fetish. *Healing Waters Floating Lamps* is a refreshing and daring breakaway from this slip shod tradition.

Acceptance of Life with its Crevices
Saktipada Patra

Kiriti Sengupta is no longer a newcomer to the portal of poetry; *The Earthen Flute* is his newest collection of verses with characteristic brilliance. Here we find a poet with a refined sensibility, a mature vision and a greater command of poetic idioms. The poems thrive in portraying emotions that in some quaint way expose the hidden beauty of the world and throw a new light on life's most common trivialities. Sengupta surveys the world about him not as a callow idealist, or as an imaginative dreamer, but as the exponent of the ethic of acceptance. All this reinforces a strange loveliness of life with its blend of worldliness and spirituality.

To explore and reveal the verses of this collection, heeding all the nuances, is to discover a particularity and a complexity of emotion. Sengupta is well aware of the importance of learning to "appreciate symbols in poetry." The novelty and the characteristic relevance of images used as symbols stimulate the readers' sensibility and understanding.

The leitmotif of the verses, as it has already been referred to, is the acceptance of life or, as Dustin

Pickering in his brilliant foreword phrases uniquely, an "affirmation of life." This is revealed in the very first poem of the collection in an oblique way and it gains in efficacy from being oblique. Sengupta here speaks of the three eyes of Durga. Obviously the third eye denotes spirituality wedded to eternity as it has been the same "over the ages." But, significantly the sculptors with their artistic vision have never bothered about it and *"They have been experimental/ Only on her earthly eyes."* They "keep an eye" (the title of the poem itself) on these eyes or take special care of them as the sculptors are concerned only about the enjoyment of earthly beauty which has its additional splendor owing to its unpredictability and infinite variety.

This perception of Nature and the world is foregrounded in "Experience Personified." Sengupta sees *"New grasses bathed/ In the dew of dawn."* He puts off his shoes, stands barefooted and walks again. He experiences an ecstasy — *"Tiny droplets envelop my feet/ And permeate the skin of my toes."* Sengupta does not call it "a feeling," he would rather name it his "experience." This is not something to be felt through the senses. Here the insentient natural world, now in tune with his feelings, takes on a personality Sengupta finds himself in communion with. The concluding lines hark back to the title and assert it.

In "Kajal Deeghi," Nature's calm is a refuge and a solace to the fretful heart: *"Leisure around the water/ It was named Kajal Deeghi."* Sengupta is reminded of Jibanananda's "Banalata Sen." The lake has, like that enigmatic maiden

Banalata, "*her profound eyes*," resembling the "*nest of a bird*" that "*house and reflect.*"

In this collection Sengupta meditates on life with dispassionate attitude (borrowed from the first poem in the series "Cryptic Idioms") knowing full well that a "balanced blend" makes "an enjoyable cocktail." (the second poem in the same series). The flute of life sounds but only to crack, and "*Religion or its absence/ Appears back to back*" (quoted from the fourth poem of the same series). The web of life is of a mingled yarn — joy and woe, good and evil, faith and skepticism woven together. The claims of total life reminding the moon with all its glory are larger than its share of "crevices" or deficiencies: "*With restricted entry of light/ Of love/ And sheer delight*" ("Moon — The Other Side").

"Time and Tide" presents a Bengali widow who "*lost her husband when she was only eighteen.*" Amidst the relentlessness and inexorability of time and tide causing the omelet to look weird, Sengupta does not fail to notice the "bright eyes" of the widow as she breaks the eggs.

Nature, an epitome of eternal life, is there as something vast and undying source of energy, consolation and wisdom. In "Womb" we find a pertinent and poignant symbol. The mother's womb refers to Mother Nature. It is clearly suggested that we are all interwoven threads in the intricate tapestry of life. Civilizational crisis lies in our disconnectedness with Nature. We shift our focus on her only after a natural disaster: "*With every earthquake I realize/ I have failed to express/ Much attention/ To my Mother.*"

The symbol of womb recurs in "Mother Water." Mother's womb is there to *"withstand much stress and strain."* The Ganga flows on *"witnessing numerous banks of civilizations"*— accommodating everything, absorbing the fallen and the dead and cleansing the earth. To this poet: *"Withdrawal has its share of symptoms/ Like a disease—"* and they both deserve care of Mother Nature (the fifth poem in the series "Cryptic Idioms"). The seventh poem of the same series reverts to the first poem of this book, The Earthen Flute. Sengupta's assertion: *"the eyes can see"* obviously suggests the third eye that opens up a *"wonderful world deep inside."* This is the "inward eye" of Wordsworth which comes to the aid of the senses that can only half perceive beauty and awakes the mind's attention to the inexhaustible loveliness and wonders of the world.

The eyes provide external stimuli, but all emotions originate from within. Sengupta's perception of life comes full circle in the concluding poem of this collection: "Struggle for Silence" in which he exalts quietude and says that life is nothing but a struggle to achieve a stage where the flute of life sounds no more to the sensual ears and one finds oneself in complete harmony with the creator: *"Quiet grandeur prevails over/ The pinnacle of worldly communion."*

Yet it is earth where the poet wishes to live bearing love in his soul ("Seventh Heaven"), the love where "I" is the nucleus. This unusual juxtaposition — self-centeredness leading to love that is usually self-effacing, leads to a complexity of emotion suggesting intimate human relationship.

In "Let The Flowers Bloom," elderly Mujibar picks both *Shapla* to be used in the kitchen and Lotus to be used in Hindu households in religious rituals. In a world, not "*broken into fragments*" (Tagore), Mujibar's little son "*stretches his brown arms in the sunlight.*" The *Tabeez* offered by the fakir embodies "*trust enriched with the flavor of innocence.*" Finally, Robi's unwavering trust breaks through the roof and some unknown bird flutters its wings satisfying his longing for the sky!

In "Reservation," Sengupta finds himself inducted into a diamond-like civilization with light of life in its core ("Yours Eternally"), but alas, even when he enjoys a happy married life in this world — being married to all its raptures, Sengupta finds his engagement ring "*put off his flesh and skin,*" but secured in the vault for him to put on again. The poem suggests his pensive regret for something missing in life; he cannot but look forward to a time in the near future when life will surely run "*gaily as the sparkling Thames*" (Matthew Arnold).

Actually in *The Earthen Flute* Sengupta is concerned with the pageant of life. The distinctive feature of his diction is density of meaning — many-levelled and metaphorical through and through. The poet achieves a rare blend of simplicity and depth with an eye for aptness and elegance barely to be found in much of the poetry written today.

The Premise of Language
Ananya S Guha

Kiriti Sengupta's *The Earthen Flute* is a collection of poems which honors the world in its multiple aspects: nature, spirituality, holy water, the river, humanism, soulfulness, materialism, one can go on. The most important and critical aspect is that Sengupta weaves this multiplicity into a complex awesome whole. This he does through short, terse statements, prose poetry and powerful narratives exploring the aesthetics of storytelling in poetry. He is not a cerebral poet; he is the poet of ether, water, earth and the senses. There is an embedded sensuousness in his poetry and especially an appeal to the tactile sense — that of touch – making him a Romantic in concern of shape and feeling. At the same time his poetry is grounded in soil — the land of Bengal with its long history of songwriters and poets.

Sengupta's poetry interrogates the premise of language. Some poems are written in snatches, some employ narratives, some take off into the world of the ordinary, and some are of spiritual intensity embodied by river, God or purely other worldly concerns. Some look at the dialectics of old age and youth, while some look at temporality — of death or even of material living. He points to a world beyond the worldly, not affecting voices of religiosity or re-birth, but a world where life has been fulfilled — the life of love, carnal desires, veneration for Him, life of the poor or the rustic, also a life of incandescent Nature. That is why one would call him a Romantic poet in the tradition of the great Romantics where idealism, pantheism and humanism work in poetic order. His post-Tagorean writing in the English language echoes Tagore's humanism and spirituality as well, all embedded in the soil, the muddy earth or the sacred rivers. Sacredness is a leitmotif in Sengupta's poetry where he upholds the interweaving of the personal and the distinctly impersonal. When he speaks of the goddess with three eyes she is impersonal being, yet human enough to arouse emotions.

Let me look at some of the individual poems. The first poem "Keep An Eye" focuses on the mythical third eye and wonders if it is a human creation or not, thus drawing a clever line between reality, myth, or imagination, a device employed by the poet now and then. In the poem "Womb" the poet talks about an earthquake and worries if Mother has been affected or not. The reference seems to be to the proverbial Mother Earth, which is the fulcrum of the universe. Mother is a metaphor for an universe tied with all life's cross currents, its "this-ness," "what-ness" something akin to Gerard Manley Hopkins' inscape and in-stress — the power of God unfailingly holding everything, every creature, every natural thing at close harmony and tandem. In "Gateway To God" there is epiphany: "*An enormous God steps in.*" Water lilies and *deeghi* sprout in his poem, "Kajal

Deeghi." Remembrances such as the mythical eyes of Banalata Sen fuse into his poetry. "Let The Flowers Bloom," as Sengupta's poetry is of the burgeoning life and the spirit — the sky, the earth and water commingling into a unity of thought and vision.

Sengupta's poetic voice remains detached; there are emotional quivers but he does not become maudlin or overtly sentimental. He is involved as a poet should be — he may use words such as "mantra" but he is not the mantric or the tantrik!

Another aspect of these poems that struck me is the distinct Tagorean world in the sense of a kind of mysticism, exhortation and transcending banalities of life. It is not a God deliverance but a God (whatever you may call Him or Her) discovery. This brings light and radiance in Sengupta's poetry. This obliterates darkness and introduces very adroitly the poetry of celebration- love, spirituality and of course the vivification of life in all its minutiae.

There is a tradition to fall back in Kiriti Sengupta's poetry. It is the tradition of the chant, the song or the *geet*. One is reminded of the chants of Mira*bai* or Kabir, this eclectic strain runs through his poems almost beatifically. Now at a time when Indian poetry in English is experimenting with words and other arts, when poetry is becoming performance, Kiriti Sengupta's poetry harks back to tradition, the tradition of the chant, the hymn, the song, yet embellishing them with a solid contemporariness. This is remarkable poetry and a gutsy breakaway from contemporary poetry, written in the English language, in India today.

A Mix of Mythology and Personal Meditations
Nathan Hassall

To neglect poetry is to neglect a fundamental aspect of the Human Condition. Poetry is a *tool* used to reflect this, a means of meshing together abstractions to create an experience of continuity. Kiriti Sengupta's *The Earthen Flute* is a carefully constructed collection of poetry which fearlessly exposes the Human Condition – brought to life visually with illustrations by the talented Tamojit Bhattacharya.

Sengupta has published eight books of poetry to date, as well as two translations. His proficiency has catapulted him into recognition in India and various international writing circles. *The Earthen Flute* is Sengupta's most recent collection of poetry and prose, which focuses sharply on the emotional aspect of the inner consciousness, using a mix of mythology and personal meditations.

On the one hand, *The Earthen Flute* plays out like a precarious melody sitting on the threshold of our perceived "World" and the "Other". This articulate collection employs intriguing whimsical poetic techniques which swing the reader into a "Higher State of Awareness". For example, in the first poem, "Keep an Eye," Sengupta references the Hindu goddess *Durga*, whose left eye connotes desire, right eye action and the central eye knowledge. The central eye is fundamental to this particular poem. Sengupta describes the eye as, "... kept open / full or half" ("Keep an Eye"), which leaves the reader contemplating a world beyond the limitations of their sensory experience. This poem is accompanied with the image of *Durga* by Bhattacharya, whose interpretation of the third eye is a white void; an open, inviting space which can only be filled by "Knowledge". This can be seen as the answer to humanity's spiritual vacuum, where one can awaken to "True Awareness". In this poem, Sengupta encapsulates delicately a statement from Plato, who believed that "Human behavior flows from three main sources: desire, emotion and knowledge." The eye is a key component of *The Earthen Flute*. It is referenced consistently in a myriad of metaphorical surroundings, as it takes on an omniscient quality, "trust me, the eye can see" ("Cryptic Idioms"). "My soul seeks, but the eyes fail to see" ("Seventh Heaven").

Occasionally, the work in *The Earthen Flute* feels overly calculated and does not suit the lucidity prominent in the rest of the collection. However, halfway through the collection, Sengupta's "Dreaming Eye" plunges the reader into an exciting chimera of surreality. In the poem, "Clues to Name," Sengupta captivates the reader with ethereal yet powerful prose. Each piece is merely titled "#" and manages to remain serene in the context of a chaotic dream. This poem is the most cryptic of the whole collection, a genuine exploration of the Self and its liberation, "Water has no call, no décor either; it floats the bone and the mortal flames free!" ("Clues to Name").

Though not often, there are times when airy overtones make it difficult to follow the flow of the poetry. I found the poem, "Womb" – a journey both personal and uncomfortable referencing the concept of birth – difficult to digest, "World, you may comment on material loss / Only the mother understands rupture pain" ("Womb"). Other times, the poetry can lack the core essence of expression, with occasional cliché phrases like, "We continue to live being frightened", ("Gateway to God") or "I don't call it a feeling, / I would rather name it / My experience" ("Experienced Personified"). These appear seldom, but are still disruptive to the reading experience. Nevertheless, these are nit-pickings against a backdrop of otherwise authentic work.

This collection pulls the reader through Sengupta's daily life as he tunes a fine juxtaposition between the outside world and the emotional side of the inner self. The strongest work which juggles the outside world and inner experience is in his short poem, "Envy", where Sengupta transcends his experiences into a metaphysical observation, "Jealous– / A Dentist can say if you are one // Your teeth deviate from / The occlusal table / And thus, lips suffer from bites" ("Envy"). This poem appears lighthearted but honest, connoting a fear of falling short of perfection – an imagery-laden treat.

Although Sengupta is not too concerned with strict rhyme schemes, the clearest use of rhyme appears in the poem, "Cryptic Idioms", "A flute sounds along the serpentine track / Breath tunes it from mute to high . . . to crack! // For eons religion or its absence / Appears back-to-back . . ." ("Cryptic Idioms"). Sengupta continues the modern tradition of free verse, not limiting himself to stricter forms of poetry. There is delicate wordplay which evokes images of a spiritually dormant world, as memory is used as a vessel, "Memories unveil themselves / Through snapshots, even / The moon has its glory / Pinned in poetry" ("Moon – The Other Side").

The Earthen Flute is a book of poetry for the spiritualist, or for someone looking to connect with their "Essential Nature". Its digestible style makes it an inviting collection for both the poetry neophyte and veteran to read. The mix of experience in the context of mythological fantasies form the basis of this intriguing collection. Sengupta begs us to use vision beyond our eyes, awareness beyond our senses, before the abruptness of our part of the Human Condition ends:

"Like an inevitable death / An enormous God steps in" ("Gateway to God").

The Earthen Flute — a review
Sunil Sharma

Words scented by belief! Words unlocking secret chambers; unclogging arteries. Words — leading to higher truths. Kiriti Sengupta is adept at opening up the potential vistas residing in the verbal structures, largely unseen.

A Bengali idol carries a different implication for the dentist from Kolkata. It becomes a new site of cultural signified for the one awakened:

Among those three eyes of Durga
The third one has been the same
Over the ages

It has been kept open
Full or half

Sculptors never bothered

They have been experimental
Only on her earthly eyes

["Keep an Eye"]

This poem contains the essence of the Kiriti oeuvre: In his avatar as a poet — a genre-bender at that — the accomplished poet skillfully separates the earthy from the divine through language, prosody and images. The iconography of the three-eyed Durga being hinted in the simple lines above is rich with history and tradition defining a community, state and a nation. Made of clay, decorated, wide-eyed, in full regalia, the goddess symbolizes the sacred feminine for the early Hindus, and, that significance accumulated over the centuries is transmitted to this day and age desiring for things divine, for a holy anchoring of existence, in the tumult of time. Brittle clay representing the power of high order! Every element surcharged with power of higher order; the humble medium depicting the holy manifestation. The Durga form combing human attributes with supernatural functions. Third eye! A source of extra information, knowledge. When open, it can remove darkness. The artist's work on the human pair of eyes, leaving this special faculty untouched. It has never varied, the symbolic eye as a sensory spring of cognition in a divine being or a highly evolved or a realized person. The third eye is the same. It is not to be altered by ordinary hands. It is a mode of seeing, organizing the reality. Kiriti suggests that art — serious art should focus on that third eye glimpsed earlier by the sages and now by a lucky few, the blessed. These truths obtained by an adept must be revealed through a proper medium. Poetry, in his case. An elevated space from where the horizon of art and science meet to collapse in order to re-form.

A dental surgeon immersed in his culture can make such subtle inter-connections between the terra firma and the ethereal. Kiriti is endowed with such a finer sensibility, an inner eye for the verities hidden from the common experience due to a tragic disconnect between the spiritual and the existential.

In a slim volume of energetic pieces — verse, prose-poems — well-produced and carrying sketches that leap out of the white backgrounds, my favorite is another gem, exploring the fluid intersection of prayer and fear of mortality. It conveys tenderly the human state at its most vulnerable; the seeking out of a superior power, of a center that can stabilize and normalize disruptions, pain and suffering; a reaching out to an invisible imagined/re-imagined in our civilizational march towards things rational. This poem epitomizes our frailties and fundamental anxieties and the mechanism to cope with impending loss and subsequent recovery — a human process achieved through the universal agency of prayer:

> *Prayers carry lives within*
> *They are expressions*
> *Our desires take refuge in—*
> *For all worldly pleasures and fulfillment*
> *We remain scared, perhaps*
>
> *Wishes are chanted with closed eyes*
> *And we continue to live being frightened*
>
> *Like an inevitable death*
> *An enormous God steps in*
> ["Gateway to God"]

In few sterling lines, Kiriti captures the mission of prayers, worldwide. Battling insecurities, physical ailments and a certain cessation, the human drama finally realizes the absence of the main protagonist, the prime mover, the origin. It is the only vehicle, sincere prayer, the humble submission that delivers us at the gateway to God. Rest on His mercy.

The Earthen Flute documents human travails and an eternal search for the divine principle for a postmodern audience busy in mass consumption. It is a return successful to our original state of being — a believer. Read it in order to get restored within by its healing touch and expression of faith in a value system, pure and simple.

The Tenets of Existentialism and Eternal Quietude
Scott Thomas Outlar

Established poet Kiriti Sengupta of Calcutta, India has teamed up with illustrator Tamojit Bhattacharya to compile a collection of short poems that, as the title indicates, focus primarily on the flesh and bone phenomenon of this earthly plane. The opening piece, "Keep An Eye," references the spiritual nature of the third eye, or what some have called the seat of the soul, but then quickly establishes the point that sculptors are not as concerned with this aspect of metaphysical consciousness as they are, instead, on experimenting with the two eyes of the actual human face. And so we know from early on that we will be taken on a journey that is influenced by those concerns which are all-too-human. This is made even clearer in the poem "Womb." Here, the female body is compared with the earth itself. An archetype that has, of course, been expressed through countless millennia by various civilizations across the planet. Such a mythos continues to ring true. There is no escaping the fundamental fact that all of us, ultimately, come from and return to the dust and dirt of terra firma.

What I found to be the most powerful poem, "Experience Personified," is a simple, serene meditation on the morning dew and the sensation it makes on one's bare feet when walking through the grass. Sengupta sums up the event:

I don't call it a feeling,
I would rather name it
my experience.

I am reminded of the birds in Aldous Huxley's book *The Island* that parrot the refrain: "Here and now, boys, here and now." This poem brings me back to the present moment with a reminder that each experience throughout the day is a reflection of eternity.

In "A Different Ballgame" Sengupta considers a problem that certain poets have encountered when realizing that their work has failed to garner attention by catching hold with reviewers. He offers two possible paths (one slightly more sarcastic than the other) that the poet can take at this stage of the process:

Redoing all your old stuff;
replacing the words
with synonyms found on Google,
or in Oxford Advanced Learners, and then submit
Them to the journals
where the editors boast about their high standards

Or

leave your old stuff as it is,
and think about the classic poets,
the masters,
who were explored
as they set out for their heavenly abode

The Earthen Flute contains a number of anecdotes pertaining to the basic routines of everyday life. In "Time And Tide" Sengupta writes about a breakfast ordered after a heavy night of drinking with friends. The cheese omelet has not been prepared correctly. When it is inquired whether the cook is new we come to discover that she is a family member of the establishment's owner who has gone through a terrible tragedy earlier in her life. The lesson this reader came away with: Let us not be aggravated by simple annoyances in life, but always remember to have compassion for those we serve as well as those who serve us.

References to both elemental and earthy ideas such as the sun, moon, lakes, ponds, birds, flowers, and the like are scattered throughout the pages, but in the final poem, "Struggle for Silence," the philosophical tenets of existentialism and eternal quietude are considered as we leave this bag of bones behind and seek harmony with the Creator. It all boils down, in the end, no matter what type of fun and games we've played here on earth, no matter how much suffering and sorrow we've experienced in this physical body, to the simple fact that entropy of the mortal coil eventually comes calling. The only question that truly matters is whether or not absolution is realized before that final bell tolls.

A Stylistic Reading of [Four] Prose Poems by Kiriti Sengupta
Susanta Kumar Bardhan

Music begins to atrophy when it departs too far from the dance; poetry begins to atrophy when it gets too far from music.—Ezra Pound

Kiriti Sengupta, a dentist by profession and literary figure by passion, has established himself as an author, poet and translator par excellence. He has penned several volumes of poems, translated Bengali poems of renowned poets into English and also aired his deep-seated, philosophically and spiritually rich personal views. All such contributions touched with down-to-earth socio-philosophical understanding and experience and intense authentic as well as aesthetic values have brought Sengupta to the limelight of contemporary literary studies both in India and abroad. His bestselling titles include *My Glass of Wine*, novelette based on autobiographic poetry, *The Reverse Tree*, nonfictional memoir and *Healing Waters Floating Lamps*, collection of poetry. Sengupta's anthology of poems *The Earthen Flute* [2016], another bestselling title in America in Indian literature, contains twenty-one poems and an incisive

214

foreword by Dustin Pickering, editor-in-chief of *Harbinger Asylum* and Founder of Transcendent Zero Press, Houston, Texas. It is no doubt a unique work in the sense that the poet's inner voice shaped by tradition, belief, experience and understanding has got due room in these poems. Dustin Pickering has rightly begun his foreword to *The Earthen Flute* titled "Dare a Poet Apologize?" by stating:

> In this small volume of delightful verses, Kiriti Sengupta speaks again of the human condition and the hidden truth of religion. The two remain inseparable in his work altogether.

The poems of the present volume address very subtle and reflective response to the issues which we face but miss due probably to our apathy or incapability to perceive. The poet, with his critical acumen and sensitivity, has aroused those before his readers. However, the present study, as the title clearly indicates, is restricted to the *four* prose poems included in *The Earthen Flute* : "Clean Gene," "Time and Tide," "Clues to Name," and "Let The Flowers Bloom" and we will basically look into how linguistic aspects have been artistically utilized to foreground the poetic message(s) in such creations.

Prose poem, as the nomenclature suggests, is basically poetic expression the medium of which is prose. Though modernist poet T. S. Eliot did not have respect for this genre, it flourished and became popular in Europe and America in the 1950s and 1960s. It is evidently a modernist-postmodernist venture on the part of artist [who practices this] to explore the multiple facets of the mystery-laden complex reality of existence and its relation with humanity at large and to reflectively as well as aesthetically give shape in a text to those. It is here relevant to quote Sengupta's reaction to this genre which he mailed to the present writer on April 18, 2017:

> Prose poems are challenging to say the least! They have an intrinsic rhythm that differentiates them from other prose works. I have seen people often refer to prose poems as prose, but prose poems are essentially poetry which employs metaphors, imagery, among other characteristics of poesy.

Before going to make the stylistic reading of the poems, let us have a brief discussion on stylistics. The first thing to notice about stylistics is that it crosses the boundaries of two academic fields: literature and linguistics. Stylistics is the scientific study of style of a literary piece with the knowledge of linguistics. It is "an attempt to criticism on a scientific basis." Stylisticians usually analyze literary texts using the tools of as well as insights from linguistics. In other words, stylistics tries to make use of the insights in linguistics to study the language of literature. We know that literature is written in language and so evidently linguistics should be able to help us understand literary texts and more importantly how we manage to understand them in the way that we do. Literary critic-linguist controversy, as we know, is found in different forums. The most well-known debate between a stylistician and a literary critic occurred between Fowler and Baetson which took place in the 1960s in the academic journal *Essays in Criticism* and its individual contributions were later gathered together in Fowler's collection of essays [Fowler 1966 & 1971]. It turned so ridiculous and ludicrous when Baetson denied to marry his sister with a linguist. Michael Short in his essay "Who is Stylistics" claims that stylistic analysis is a considerable advance on the main teaching strategy of literary criticism, because it helps us explain how people understand particular texts. Mere linguistic description of a literary text is not the aim of stylistics. It attempts to relate that with the meaning of effect of the text. It helps us arrive at a description which, to some extent, eliminates the need of impressionistic value based judgments. It is objective and precise in methods of description leading to interpretation. In order to substantiate the relationship between literature and linguistics we can quote great British scholar Leech's [1969] comment regarding this:

> By popular definition, literature is the creative use of language, and this in the context of general linguistic description can be equated with the use of unorthodox or deviant forms of language.

1

Clean Gene

Rina works as a therapist in a beauty salon. Her office enjoys a nation-wide network, and now they wish to reach out to global customers. Rina meets her clients, she talks to them and listens to the problems they are suffering from. She lends patient hearing and her skilled suggestions are well received. Rina has a radiating skin that often fetches compliments...

During a client meet someone inquired, "Rina, you look so gorgeous. Did you ever have an acne or two?" Rina took no time to answer, "You know, I'm genetically blessed with a clean skin!"

The poem "Clean Gene" is thematically an outcome of the interaction between a therapist in a beauty salon, Rina, and her client. Rina who *"has a radiating skin that often fetches compliments ..."* serves her client patients with care and her *"skilled suggestions are well received."* In response to a client's question relating to gorgeous acne-free beauty, she spontaneously answers, *"You know, I am genetically blessed with a clean skin!"* The poem apparently seems to be common and a simple discourse. At the deeper level, it is highly loaded with cultural, sociological and psychological suggestions conveyed through the skillful use of day-to-day language.

Notice: The first and second stanzas differ in the usage of tense. While the events in the first one have been described in simple present tense, those in the second [excluding the speeches] in simple past tense. The second stanza depicts one specific interaction occurred in one particular day and it is encapsulated by the regular activities as represented by the use of simple past tense. The dominant use of two basic sentence types Subject-Verb-Complement [SVC] and Subject-Verb-Object [SVO] significantly projects the event closer to a common man's experience. Two relative clauses, one "they are suffering from" employed to modify the head NP [Noun Phrase] "the problems [of the patient clients)" and the other "that often fetches compliments..." employed to modify the head NP "a radiating skin [of Rina]," bear parallel load to draw the contrast inherent in the poem. Moreover, the sign of ellipsis [three dots] after "compliments" in "that often fetches compliments…" leads the readers to assume what they can. Such open-ended expression, indicated by sign of ellipses and rising tone [Rising tone is used to indicate incompleteness], makes the discourse poetically sound.

Again, this open-ended discourse gets mystified and heightened when the poem ends with Rina's deep faith-and-conviction-born prompt utterance: *"You know, I am genetically blessed with a clean skin!"* The first part of it "You know," seems to have created a very casual and non-serious atmosphere, but that has been dispelled by the immediately following passive complement clause. The agent of *blessing* here remains unidentified and the adverb "genetically" also asserts the conscious knowledge of the speaker. The usage of rising tone in the first part and falling tone [Falling tone is used to indicate assertion and completeness] in the second/last part of the utterance are contrastive but conclusive in terms of poetic message. All such linguistic devices have been utilized to foreground the semantically loaded image when both conscious and unconscious merge.

2

Time And Tide

It was 8 am and the butler inquired, "What would you like to have for your breakfast, Sir?" We partied last night with a group of young ladies. We had good food with plenty of drinks. I cautiously ordered a slice of bread and a cheese omelet. I heard the boy instructing a woman-cook. It was an open kitchen arrangement, and I saw a Bengali widow in her late forties placing the bread-slice in the toaster. She set the time and quickly picked two eggs from the basket. I noticed her bright eyes as she broke the eggs.

The boy served me breakfast on a white dish. The bread was perfect, but the omelet looked weird. I could make out the woman did not whisk the yolks properly. A bit annoyed with the quality of service, I asked the waiter, "Is she a new appointee?" He hesitantly replied, "She is my aunt, Sir. She lives in our ancestral home and she lost her husband when she was only eighteen!"

The prose poem "Time and Tide" records the poet speaker's stay in a hotel, having previous night party and morning breakfast comprising bread and omelet. In the midst of all these, a widow, in her late forties who was engaged in cooking, drew the attention of the speaker who "*noticed her bright eyes as she broke the eggs.*" He was convinced that the woman "*did not whisk the yolks properly*" and so it looked weird. This led him to inquire about the widow: "Is she a new appointee?" The waiter informed him that she was his aunt who lost her husband at the age of eighteen. With the statement of the waiter giving the information about the ill-fated girl-turned-widow-turned-cook, the poem ends leaving multi-faceted deeper sensations in the form of *byanjanaa* or *dhwani* (suggestion).

The very title of the poem "Time and Tide" links its implicitly stated message with eternity and eternal truth relating to all-powerful TIME which crushes and engulfs everything unknowingly and unfailingly. The mere description of the night party and breakfast creates the foundation on which the widow with bright eyes engaged in preparing "weird" omelet as a part of speaker's breakfast has been placed. The entire event is the past one as conveyed by the use past tense in the whole discourse excluding the reporting speeches. Most of words and the derivatives are common. But see that the noun 'appointee' is not very common and so the question "Is she a new appointee?" uttered with rising tone bears significance and signification to the addressee, here the waiter. Hence instead of answering 'Yes' or 'No' to this *polarity type* question, the waiter details her past and present life, a tragic one as indicated by very emotionally charged intonation pattern and by the use of noun phrases such as "my aunt," "our ancestral house," "her husband," and lastly "only eighteen." The poem, though apparently prosaic in form, is charged with maximum meaning conveyed through every bit of image-creating expression.

3

Clues To Name

An experiment I undertook. A seed slept in dark, clueless; no viable chant ... what if awakened by a mantra? A syllable to prefix and suffix, and thus was my pride and prejudice! Got confined, even as I wish to move on. Now the pride is dear; dearer than my dearest...

#

Following some cunning way I was keen to taste some greatness. A tree stands with its green veil. Through its branches I noticed the ascent of sap, but it had no salt. Some names sweet ... some seeds added at source!

#

As one finds it apt! Just the way the mind seeks. My mind. Mantra bears lust ... petty you, you blame the luster! Lust reinstated ... inevitable it is...

#

Immersion via the mirror ... goodbye to the goddess, but the lion keeps awake with his eyes closed. His eyes are terrific ... mesmerizing, or giving all as I surrender. The first involves mixing while the latter denotes craving!

#

Deviations bring popularity ... endless celebrations. Fists full of water and free donation ... serving the pilgrims. Withdrawal reversed...

#

Complete bath and a full dip ... no excuses, please ... be it the pollution sick! You sprinkle drops, however ... your wisdom runs into the lustrous hole. Incenses are not burnt by wet hands, they say. Prohibited it is. Water has no call, no décor either; it floats the bone and the mortal frames free!

"Clues to Name" consists of six stanzas which appear to be incoherent, disjointed and full of concrete images. The six stanzas stand out to be separate six poems dealing with the dormant and later awakened seed, flow of sap within a tree, inevitability and renewal of lust leading luster, immersion of Goddess, not of her bearer lion, celebration of [religious] festival and the power of water without name ["call"] and color ["décor"] to make the mundane existence free ["*it floats the bone and the mortal frames free!*"]. However, all these stanzas are interlinked, intertwined and interwoven through the central images i.e., seed and water. The poems demand from the reader several rounds of reading for enjoying the poetic idea spread as an undercurrent throughout the text.

The very first sentence of the poem having the object NP "An experiment" at the topic position sets the idea that the poet speaker 'undertook' a journey of experimentation running throughout the text. The very mode, process and mood of experimentation which is sometime spontaneous and sometime proceeds with halts and pauses [shorter or longer] can be traced and perceived in the poetic use of verbless expressions or clauses having only NPs and fourteen inter-sentential and inter-clausal gaps indicated by the signs of ellipses each. Unuttered messages are born out of such crevices, created and generated by such (non-)linguistic devices. The dynamic interplay of rising and falling tones in the entire text superimpose and intensify the artifact.

"*A syllable to prefix and suffix*" carries metaphorical and synecdochic implications as a *name* 'sweet' consists of syllable[s] and this name assignment demands clues or hints or associations grown out of cultural, religious, psychological [dis]beliefs and [dis]likes. Hence, to the poetic self, "*Now the pride is dear; dearer than my dearest...*" and so NP 'the pride' is no more an abstract but intensely connotes a concrete perceptible one as conveyed by elliptical NP 'my dearest ...' without the head noun. Surface appearance of every earthly living entity is the result of *in stress* inherent in seed germinated to grow with a name. The mystery of birth and growth i.e., creation has been aptly conveyed by the last line of the second stanza: "*Some names sweet ... some seeds added at source!*' consisting of only two NPs containing postmodifiers 'sweet' and 'added at source' leading to the structure: NP-S [rel. clause].

Interestingly the poem takes a turn after the second stanza. First two stanzas describe the past experiment and experience, the remaining four stanzas, present event-cum-experiments leading the poet to a poetically sound psycho-philosophical plane. Thus, the tense-and-time use in the whole poem functions as a linguistic vehicle to suggest that our encounters with the day-to-day events or facts are restricted not only to past time or to only present time, but to the past-and-present continuum leading to future mystery.

In the third stanza the occurrence of only NP 'My mind' in the sentence without verb focuses the absolute authority or independence of poet's mind in thinking, feeling, understanding and all kinds of mental activity. The three-word clause/sentence 'Mantra bears lust' emerges as a powerful statement to highlight the convergence and confluence of the unconscious desire projected as lust' and the conscious action chanting 'mantra' driven by lust. Reinstatement and inevitability of 'lust' have been markedly projected by NP 'Lust reinstated' having NP-S structure followed by three dots followed by clause 'inevitable it is' in which the predicative adjective 'inevitable' has been put in the topic position and then followed by three dots. These devices have, as we see, been utilized to put forward the very life force represented by 'lust.

The lion which acts as the *bahana* [bearer] of the goddess immersed via mirror emerges as the symbol all sorts of craving generated by the unconscious identified with lust. See, the fifth stanza, which states about the contemporary trends in festival celebration, consists of one finite clause or sentence followed by four verb-less small clauses connected by dots. This depicts the sporadic ideas occupying the poet's mind struggling frantically to share with his reader.

In the concluding sixth stanza 'water' gains the symbolic significance as *"it floats the bone and the mortal frames free!"* The two NPs 'the bone' and 'the mortal frame' have been used to mean the same i.e., human body born out of lust, luster and above all seed or embryo. Simultaneous use of synecdoche, metonymy and metaphor uniquely projects the idea that it is water which ultimate liberates or mind or soul from the corporeal entity.

4

Let The Flowers Bloom

Elderly Mujibar has no money; he owns a hovel and a large pond. Mujibar eats rice and boiled Shapla as he returns from work. He grows Shapla in the pond that also has Lotus in it. Mujibar picks both the flowers and keeps them in bunches before he vends the flowers in the market. His five-year-old son fails to understand which bunch will be used in their kitchen and what goes into the Hindu household.

\#

A white Lotus turns red as the Sun rises high in the sky. Mujibar has no clue to the occurrence, and considers it a phenomenon. His little son rushes to the veranda and stretches his brown arms in the sunlight.

\#

Leaving behind his little son alone Mujibar dies of uncontrolled fever! In the afternoon the small boy wanders around the paddy field, and in the morning he works in the tea-stall adjacent to his hut. He serves tea in small glasses to the customers.

\#

The small boy grows up a bit; people call him by the name Robi. On a chilly winter morning a fakir arrives at the tea-stall. He does not have warm clothing. Robi approaches the fakir, "My father has given me a roof, but I have no sky to look at."

\#

The fakir offers a tiny copper-box, a tabeez, *which is considered holy. He suggests, "Chain it around your neck, my son!" Robi protests, "Hey, you gave me a piece of copper while I asked for the sky?" The fakir urges enthusiastically, "Come on, it is filled with my prayers. I have given you a mountain, rather, and now you break through the roof you have."*

\#

No magic, but sheer trust enriched with the flavor of innocence! Robi does not work anymore; he enjoys a never ending stay in his hut as he cherishes the saintly mountain. The roof remains unchanged; the moon does not arrive. A slice of the sky does not even appear despite Robi's uninterrupted wanting for it. He holds the tabeez *tightly in his grip, and while looking at the roof he murmurs, "I won't offer you a drape if I don't get a bird."*

\#

A bird flutters its wings and the sound is pretty familiar. Not a crow, nor a heron — some unknown bird. It keeps standing in the mud-pad. A few flowers are visible, and they are not Shapla. *Robi feels warm, his arms, especially the spine region, as if there is a sudden rush of hot water along the spinal duct!*

\#

A fragrant ambience sets in while the bird floats up in the air. Robi's face attracts drops of mud from the flying bird. Handful of soil and the hut is flooded with sunlight that enters from the broken roof. Robi feels much warmer now. A milkman knocks the door, "Store milk in the can, chacha!*"*

We shall now proceed to study the last poem of our present attempt and it is "Let The Flowers Bloom." Here we shall quote Dustin Pickering's comments about the present poem in the foreword:

> The collection is not nearly as simple as it appears. Let's take a look at "Let The Flowers Bloom". The prose poem is highly symbolic of Indian history. This piece is small miracle of literature. Ultimately, the young boy recalls an Indian of the copper age. The Continent hasn't been the same after Partition. Bangladesh and

India, once of the same continent, currently shaped by relations of either-or. Sometimes accepting each other as neighbors and at other moments falling into disputes over immigration, the Ganges River waters that Bangladeshis feel robbed of, border disputes, the shortsighted statement of political leaders, or several others things that stir tension, Bangladesh and India are still part of the same soul. The symbolic use of familiar "Uncle" expresses a sense of discontinuity - who is India really? Partition and religious conflict wrecked the continent, confusing identity. Sengupta assesses the problem fairly in other parts of the collection, as in "Do You Have a Christian Name?"

The eight-stanza poem which depicts briefly the eights glimpses of the events relating to the life of the young boy, Robi, encompasses a wide span of time and so it enjoys the status of a narrative poem marked by brevity and symbolic dimension. The flowers *shapla* (white lily) and lotus Mujibar grows in his pond and vends them in the market symbolically represent food for Muslims and means of Hindu worship respectively. The two nominal complement clauses "which bunch will be used in their kitchen" and "what goes in into the Hindu household" connected by conjunction 'and' function as the object of the verb 'understand' and thus, reveal the fundamental reality of rural Bengal life. The very change of white lotus into red one in the sunlight remains a mystery to Mujibar's son for whom more mystery-ridden life awaits. The death of his father forces him to work in the paddy field and tea stall for his livelihood. Here

Robi's afternoon activity i.e., wandering in the paddy field has been put first and then his morning activity i.e., serving in the tea-stall. This change of normal order [i.e., morning followed by afternoon] intensifies the sorrow-and-poverty ridden life of an orphan. As the time passes, Robi grows not only physically but also socially and spiritually as evidenced by his simple but highly philosophical appeal to the fakir: "*My father has given me a roof but I have no sky to look at.*" The fall-rise tone in the first independent clause and falling tone in the second one deepen the situation the boy is destined to be in. Fakir's offering of copper *tabeez* containing his prayer to Robi generates in him the "*sheer trust enriched with the flavor of innocence*!" See that first line of the sixth stanza contains two NPs connected by adversative conjunction 'but' and make the reader predict what is going to happen as well as develop the unspoken in his/her mind.

In course of time the appearance of "*some unknown bird*" which "*keeps standing in the mud-pad*" and the sight of a few flowers, not *shapla*, make Robi feel warm. When the bird flies up in the sky and sunlight enters in to the hut through the broken roof, he feels much warmer and a milkman appears with milk. In the entire discourse the flower, bird and milk gradually gain symbolic dimension so far as the portrayal of tragic life of a boy. The modulation of tone and rhythm in the text aptly portrays the trajectory of the intensive growth of the artifact.

Note that the use of local Bangla words, instead of using their English counterparts, has authentically retained the local or regional flavor, taste and culture and the semantic load of these words remain intact in the texture and structure of the text. The poet, Sengupta, has shown his sense of economy in the use of such local words.

To conclude the above discussion on the four prose poems of Kiriti Sengupta from the perspective stylistics has exhibited several stylistic devices effectively used in these poems with a view to foregrounding the poetic messages and raising the poems to the heightened level of art, in the true sense of the term. It is also necessary to note that Sengupta has composed and published in the recent past a collection of eighteen prose poems titled *Reflections on Salvation* [2016] dealing with different aspects of *Moksha Yoga* as dealt with in the concluding chapter of *The Geeta*. These poems need to be studied separately from the stylistic point of view and that work is being kept for future venture.

Works Cited

Fowler, R. (ed.) *Essays on Style and Language*. London: Routledge & Kegan Paul Ltd. [1966].
The Linguistics of Literature. London: Routledge & Kegan Paul Ltd. [1971].
Leech G.N. *A Linguistic Guide to English Poetry*. London and Harlow: Longsman, Green and Co. Ltd. [1969].
Pickering, Dustin. "Dare a Poet Apologize?" Foreword to Kiriti Sengupta's *The Earthen Flute*. Kolkata: Hawakal Publishers 2016.
Sengupta, Kiriti. *The Earthen Flute*. Kolkata: Hawakal Publishers 2016.
Sengupta, Kiriti. *Reflections on Salvation*. Texas: Transcendent Zero Press. 2016
Short, M. "Who is Stylistics" *Focus on English* Vol. 1, No. 3. 2-22. 1985.
Widdowson, H. G. *Stylistics and the Teaching of Literature*. London: Longman. 1975.

The Earthen Flute — A Flux of Contraries
Tuhin Sanyal

In popular belief, 'Mysticism' is 'unifying with God or the absolute,' or even unifying with the ecstatic or the altered state of consciousness. It is often given a religious or spiritual meaning vide epiphanies or revelations and inspired interpretations of the world-order and other mumbo-jumbo in relation to the Godly. But definitions change; and the mannerisms of exacting ideas and definitions, in relation to contemporariness, egg on the Human Being to search for a New Expression for Old Clichés — coherent and topical with his times. From this dialectical pattern, the new poet who is born after the death of God, starts legislating. Where the Godly ends, his Poetry begins. Devoid of the Godly authority, his legislations become the harbingers of expressions that are blinding paradoxes for innovative introspection. In that vein, the problem in relation to Mysticism and mystical experience created terrorizing tremors in the Richter Scale of human psyche ever since the death of God, and birth of Blake. Nietzsche furthered the truth about God's death all the more with his path-breaking theories of annihilation—psychological theories, backed by the pseudo-scientific (logical-rhetorical-metaphorical) plausibility of existentialism, theories of all gods in fortuitous circumstances, and their resultant deaths accruing thereof. In such Godless times, the Romantic Blake automatically became foregrounded as the messiah or poet-prophet since he could refer to the attainment of insight in ultimate or intuitive hidden truths, and to human transformation supported by the paradoxical commonality of human experiences.

I am not too much of a God-fearing man; to me God is not (m)aligned with orthodox Religion, Cult or Order, but to me 'god' is a way of life, 'religion' is anything pertaining to Humanity, and 'cult' is sheer Practice of the commune. And to me, all of that amount to Poetry. I am an avid reader of *good* poems (Pray, do not dub me value-judgmental yet!), I try my hand at writing good verses (I too am an 'unacknowledged legislator!'), and I am always on the lookout for new books of verses that may appeal to my mind and body alike (Pray, also do not dub me a sensual, pseudo-intellectual!). The other day, while traversing and tripping through the 'virtual' world and its pseudo-poetic drudgery, I suddenly was able to lay my hands (not feet, since I knelt down to pick it up the moment it saw it!) on a book of 'real' poetry. The poet had three 'I's (read 'eyes') in his first name — K-I-R-I-T-I — *Kiriti Sengupta!* Two eyes are always fine; but I felt inquisitive to know if the poet truly had his third-'I/eye' in place, and whether he could see the *Discordiaconcors* of the world-(dis)orders with that Instrument of Intuition and Intention which creates a poet. Thankfully the justified 'I/eye'-conscious in his poems did not dishearten me!

It seemed to me that much of the book was meant 'to conceal' than reveal flat and point-blank natural, liturgical, spiritual, and contemplative dimensions of the human cravings from poetry. It had its own crypts and cryptic codes. On making a careful scrutiny of the initial pages, I found that the poet with three 'eyes/I's— KIRITI—had quite audaciously dedicated the book to William Blake. Audacity? Not really! Such audacity is quite just when his poetic intuition is able to ken the "Gateway to God" (Pp.25) and yet *"continue to live being frightened,"* sustain life somehow, much like Rintrah in Blake's "The Marriage of Heaven and Hell." Ironically, and yet keeping in sync with the foregone discussion, in a queer Blake-ian pattern Kiriti upholds his range of religio-rational beliefs and ideologies, related to the extraordinary experiences and states of his individual moral code, which prompt him to "Keep An Eye" (Pp.15), *"the third one"* in particular, *"over the ages"* about which *"sculptors never* (actually) *bothered"*. Unwittingly perhaps, the poet reiterates Blake's vision of the brooding abyss of the Universe dominated by Urizen (I decode the crypt as 'Your Reason') who keeps vigil on the 'contraries' that lead to 'progression'— a progression through contraries, which other poets and sculptors, except Blake, could not conceive of.

Interestingly enough, Blake was a sculptor himself and he chiseled the first manuscript of *Songs of Innocence* with his own hand, much as a collage of glue-papyrus-metals, adding natural dyes as colors, to give it the shape of a book of apparently simplistic rhymes, which would later be telling upon the much dogmatic Christian religious order of the times. The cliché of world's experiment with the *"earthly eyes"* of *Durga* (name of a Mother-Goddess of the Hindu pantheon), negates a sacrament in the superimposition of a living human non-entity (a sundry woman by the same name) and the lifeless Godly entity by the very appellation. To add to this, such experiment is thoughtless, audacious, marginalizing, as well as pathetic in terms of the indifference of creative artists. Kiriti challenges the hollow, pseudo-religious throe in dogmas (here, 'experimenting' is one such), just as Blake had challenged Swedenborg. But Kiriti chooses to express with a postmodernist's insight, from his Indian ethos, though in a clear parallel with Blake's displaced Jehovah and Christ as the 'Son of God' (not God Himself) — an oblique fling of the dogmatic Christian pantheon.

The poet of *The Earthen Flute* pipes to his readers very simple (though seemingly problematized), earthly—hence factual—ditties just as Blake would by juxtaposing 'innocence' and 'experience'. Kiriti, like Blake, too believes in the reinstatement of contraries of good and evil side by side, since that is the inevitable actuality; and he has his "Clues to Name" (Pp.31-32). In this new world order of C.2016, he makes a clean breast of *"Lust reinstated… inevitable it is…"* which undergoes *"Immersion via the mirror…* (and bids) *goodbye to the goddess"*, notably, with a small 'g'. In an accepted (Hindu) ritualistic bid the Goddess Durga, as in Kiriti's poem, is first immersed in the liquid haze of a mirror (symbolic of water or River Ganga); lust of the male gaze is already reinstated therein, but is hinted at as if through cryptic language, until the post-consummation final 'goodbye' is bid to the 'goddess', only too fit for earthly consummation—

a 'goddess' (diva?) with a real body to forebode issues of gender. In "The Marriage of Heaven and Hell" Blake visualizes the *The Holy Bible* on the library shelf of 'The Devil'. God, for Blake, is Urizen ('your reason' with an imperfect 'U' lacking closure) and, to some extent, Jehovah, who can also be malevolent. Kiriti re-does a Blake's in the same throe which amalgamates reason and 'practiced' religion in its fold, but with a difference. He does not sound prophetic, and his poems are not sermons. In a way, Kiriti speaks of a natural religion that is Man!

"Mother Water" (Pp.51) recurs in the "Nucleus" (Pp.42) of Kiriti's poetry, and he adds ripples to it with the vibes of *The Earthen Flute*. "*Ganga has her stories to tell… (she) listens to our prayers / Both mute and loud.*" The queer 'flux' of 'opposites' wrench his expressions out from a poetic 'fixity' which is his own. Sometimes they are ace ironies in themselves; just as the "Womb," for him, is akin to and reminiscent of the archetypal "*earthquake.*" He is religio-rational, just like Blake's first person narrator Rintrah, thinking aloud while visit to Hell is still on. Hell is not seen as a place of punishment, which is obviously the common association to it, but it is seen as a source of unrepressed feelings, creative energy, and personal-spiritual progression. Similarly, Kiriti's womb — earthquake (birth — devastation) equation is an opposing and oblique, as well as a regulated and authoritarian perception of heaven-in-hell and hell-in-heaven, as if in a Blakeian bid to reiterate Milton's and Dante's thoughts in their great works. With this, Kiriti becomes a serious dissenter, who is permanently searching for a neo-modern, neo-mystic and neo-spiritual, practicable poetic truth by marrying off the contraries or the opposites. His *The Earthen Flute*, apparently a title with a low-key note, basks in the pathos of burning water (much like a romantic oxymoron) where "*No ash is formed.*" It gives its readers beauty, reminds them of some faraway music, the smell of the rain drenched earth, first love, the empty eve of *Durga Dashami* (after Goddess Durga is immersed in the river), a sexual aftermath, *"gathering swallows twitter(ing) in the skies,"* or, say, a *"sunny pleasure dome with caves of ice,"* but with a postmodernist's expression.

A Poet in Search of Unity in Existential Disjoints

P C K Prem

To collect memories, experiences and impressions in little fragments has moments of joy and anguish because totality or conclusiveness in invisible and indefinite regions of feelings and abstractness remains indistinct and vague. Crisis in current life does not permit time to the artist to organize and manage cacophonous notes in life's activities. Therefore, contradictions and inconsistencies, distress even as disunity in creativity stays firm. A search for unity and harmony in disturbed times is the artist's worry to avoid post-modernistic disquiet and paradox and hence, to locate "existential silence" ("Struggle For Silence") in life is the objective the poet aspires for obliquely notwithstanding the survival of eternal questions he raises.

Someone inquired if I was aware of existential silence...
But then, how do people perceive quietude?
Is it a state of complete absence of noise?
Does clamor invite peace, by any chance?

The Earthen Flute raises such questions and makes efforts to find cogent answers. To construct what happened just a few moments ago in the past defies precision. If to give a structure to experiences is difficult, to offer a palpable meaning to vivid sketches and paintings is also not a very convenient proposition. One is sure to confront multiple definitions and confounding possibilities of defining the abstract in language. When Kiriti, as a poet, attempts to fathom the mystic of experiences, he drives everyone to bewildering and esoteric newness that confuses, irritates and questions the wisdom of man. The uniqueness of interpreting experiences, memories and impressions lies in the truth that he relates little bit of every area to existence, history, legends and myths. He is not direct but distantly defines borders of experiences and everything he encounters as intangible and indistinct.

If in *Healing Waters Floating Lamps* Kiriti is unusual in poetic art, and loves to recreate experiences and analogous baffling imitations and puts stress on understanding, his imaginative engagement in the re-creation process with familiar words gives birth to quaintly untried situations and experiences as one encounters in contemporary life. *Healing Waters Floating Lamps* "demonstrates experiential and experimental proclivity even toward different characters no doubt, without apparent prejudice but still gets dissolved in 'the self'… he does not adhere to one ultimate meaning he wishes to convey through the text but one finds deconstruction quite active and it offers varied meanings, some so clear on surface and a few meanings seem conditional." However, in *The Earthen Flute*, Kiriti is a little unambiguous and endeavors to lessen the indistinctness lyrics create.

The Earthen Flute, is a lyrical journey from the disturbed 'outside' to the 'the inside world' that opens up possibility of granting some solace to a man in search of harmony in the contemporary world, and in doing so, it enlarges the canvas. Man often ignores the implicit or the faint and if he goes deep, he is only experimental. The real meaning is apparent only when man comprehends the mystery before the obvious. If he hints at the third eye in "Keep An Eye," it is the divine prowess that notices what man hides within. A poet conveys the message symbolically and leaves an imprint. In "Womb," the mother stands for creation, preservation and endurance and thus, if mother (the woman) and earth (the mother) are guardians of the niceties of cultural heritage, then mother as a woman hints at an inextricable relationship with the man notwithstanding diversities in outlook. The third eye also speaks of the divine blessing on humankind notwithstanding any thought of virtue or sin. *Durga*, as a goddess has many images, of them nine are significant, which Hindus think as the creators, guardians of the ethics and the virtuous and the destroyers of sinners but he does not tell and so, asks man to make an inquiry. The poet sensitively speaks of modern consciousness where man is worried about poverty, hunger and scarcities that make life difficult. Social issues perturb but he is never obvious ("Moon — The Other Side")

A tombstone may ask for
Flowers and your tears,
While frank hunger can only be fed
By some food to eat
If you can remember,
Even the moon has its share of crevices

Experiences carry different shades of feelings elusive but infuse amiability and pleasantness unparalleled. If earlier, he compares "profound eyes" with "the nest of a bird" and obliquely speaks of intensity of thoughts where man often seeks asylum in crisis and thus, tacitly tells of woman's identity, firm and rock-hard. "In Experience Personified," he touches with tender feelings as if.

Tiny droplets envelop my feet
And permeate the skin of my toes
I don't call it a feeling,
I would rather name it
My experience

It is an invite to feel the soothing touch of dew as you walk on the grass. Maybe it is a message a man ought to listen to when nature is intimate and yet far away. Undercurrent of irony, a bit of humor and incisiveness in the expression of failure makes "A Different Ballgame" quite realistic and contemporary.

Fragmentary encounters with fractured experiences testify poet's keenness in discerning something people often ignore or perhaps do not think of sagacious bearing. Random thoughts and ramblings in the process of concretizing even if prosaic make a sensible impression but fail to carry further. The poet intentionally indulges in the pleasure of straight sentences or maybe he wants us to split each sentence to give meaning. The poet usually makes a detour and if he satisfies a bit with certain observations, he irritates with obviously confounding propositions, and the technique provokes in "Clues to Name," for at times, gaps and blanks give plethora of inapt connotations and unmeaning inappropriate, at times.

Kiriti plays with the words astutely and in the pleasure of diversion, distortion in objective surfaces. However, the lines simply engage and befuddle with the resonance the words create. At such junctures, poetry should not only appease the connoisseurs of poetic art, the intellectuals or the urban thinkers but also reach the poetry lovers, who enjoy even at the risk of not understanding it suitably. Import of many meanings is good but its layers of meanings crush the poetic principle and the solemn objective of the bard.

Deviations bring popularity ... endless celebrations. Fists full of water and free donations ... serving the pilgrims. Withdrawal reversed...

It appears a premeditated attempt where the poet wants to mystify and confound, and therefore, abandons the clarity and generates cracks and disunity in poetic space. It appears he fails in what he wishes to say in verses and therefore, creates not exactly haziness in genres but deliberately turns to prose-like statements. Not many lyricists have indulged in the luxury of mixing up different genres to expound dilemmas of cloudy experiences, which however, defy wholeness in phrase. If he irritates, he wishes to fulfill intent unstipulated. Alternately, he compensates in "Cryptic Idioms" where he defines the limits of traditionalist or non-conformist meaning whether perceptible or otherwise.

I say Yama and you think of
The god of death
I said Yama,
But I meant the laws of restraint.

The spectacle of lines and innate meaning captivate and that speaks of poet's awesome lyrical skill. His poetry elevates because it does not sermonize. Again, he surprises with the finely weaved rhythmic lines, "*Withdrawal has its share of symptoms / Like a disease- / They both deserve care; they prefer / Nature, countryside over metropolis.*" Depiction of social responsiveness and contemporary anxieties find meticulous expression without hurt feelings but union of unsystematic notions give rise of varied meanings that keep integral the curiosity to go beyond the apparent meaning.

A thought or perhaps a feeling to expand, distresses because when a man carries the burden of fixation, a care for self-image, it gives birth to evil tendencies and a man scarcely opens to humanistic regions of meaningful life. If, in materialistic living, thoughts of the eternal crop up, in a strange twist of upsurge of thoughts and feelings, nostalgic moments take the man to ancestors, people, who are no more on earth but the past at the particular slice of time definitely rejuvenates ("Nucleus").

Tiny pieces of chocolate live in the cookies
And when they surface
I call it "hide and seek"
There is an old woman with her older man
In the vast of the sky
While the stars smile and twinkle.

The image of cookies not only hints at some moments of joy in the past but the poet's reluctance or possibly lack of recognition talks of 'an old woman' and 'older man' but even without acceptance he seems to go back to reflective chapters of life that remain in memory. He wishes to grant immortality to the souls, who are no more and somewhere he connects 'the self' to past so that he derives identity but refuses to agree. Man often speaks of relations and warmth but in reality, self-interest and self-centeredness determine life.

When relations sustain, pecuniary structure takes care and that is what he callously tells in "Reservation" (*I enjoy a happy married life / But then, very few of us / Take care of our fingers*). If one goes back, relations tread the same path with minor adjustments, for survival is the core, "*I won't even try the lane that does not lead to your home -/ No matter if you say this for several times / My heart beats faster or slower than the normal rate…*" It indicates compulsiveness in human bonds and tenuous efforts to hold on to it look skeptical.

The mind and heart of a man never permits to stay in a particular region and loves to grow, expand and exist in each particle of life because he begins to look at life everywhere and so he feels it. "Let the Flowers Bloom" metaphorically tells of a refuge, a guardian and a guide and of a seeker and an enquirer, who lives and suffers, and is quite conscious of the contemporary sufferings. It is hard work and still faith in the superstitious that work as props to make life beautiful, for everyone has his share of sky. Man ought to keep hopes alive and live. *Robi* is the future and if, the poet appears to suggest, man takes care of the buds, garden of humankind would allure. It is also pure economics of life, for if provinces in which a man survives provide minimum comforts, it signals the fulfillment of obligatory duties a man has. It keeps the life in motion and the thought in a slightly different way appears in "(Un)Timely Grant." A living being must live life with a purpose and then, reflect over the deemed purpose (perhaps futility) and abdicate so that someone else takes over.

Prose and poetry intermingle, and offer glimpses of poet's predicament as to how best he can say what he intends telling. When Kiriti emerges out of ambiguity and vacillation, perhaps he would be straight…but alas! He does not want and that way he makes everyone scratchy. One must accept the truth that situation, location and the undefined zone where a man breathes has its own limits. You go with a thought and come back with a similar intent. It makes you impatient but you cannot reach a viable outcome. It limits the creative artist but not the art. "Mother Water" celebrates the beauty, majesty and eternal worth of River Ganga, a symbol of ancient culture, civilization and heritage. Ganga is the mother, an embodiment of revitalizing energy that remains an invisible entity but its water, a metaphor for the whole of water in the world, proves a nectar, for sans water one cannot imagine life. It takes a man back to *Puranic* legends and myths and one tries to find a godly affiliation as legendary Bhagirath, Dilip and Sagar flash on the memory chart and that makes the lyric impressive.

Ganga has her stories to tell
Wish she had someone to listen to her
Story of her nursing the fetus
Contained in an inflated uterus
While patiently awaiting her tour
Accompanying the new life.

Linking contemporary anxieties, an inquisitiveness to look beyond the apparent realities, religious faith and spiritual disquiet to life and existence on earth give extra strength to poet's lyrics, which require insight to go beyond what he really tells when he reenergizes and relives memories and experiences. He struggles to figure out the intangible in language. He is precise but still many flaws in expression haunt because he wishes to speak of reality and then, tries to go beyond reality so that he witnesses its real face but plain simulation surfaces, for it becomes awfully hard rather impossible to give language, style and frame to surrealistic tendencies. However, it is not poet's weakness but it is obviously an impractical proposition to catch hold of the shadows and the indefiniteness in meaning and shape experiences create, as a man moves from 'the inside' to 'the outside' world.

Not Just another Writer among the Mass
Koushik Sen

Kiriti Sengupta's newest chapbook, *Reflections on Salvation*, is plain interesting, for it is interesting when a dental surgeon looks on at his city with zealous eyes his observations are seated in quotidian life; they are not at all pedantic, and offers a free and unfettered reading (I hope this staves off the fear of reading another religious discourse based on faith which keeps reason at a safe distance. Footnotes are a rarity; you won't require answering the bell at the bottom of the page while making love to the content above).

In the passages that Sengupta pens in this book, we get a glimpse of the anger that breathes like ember in the mind of a man who is hell bent on reason, and not blindly following in the dictum of god-men. As Dr. Casey Dorman writes in the foreword to this volume: "His beautiful small book, *Reflections on Salvation*, wrestles with the conflict between the strict scriptural (i.e. *The Geeta*) interpretation of salvation that recognizes that it may represent different things for different people, including the massive number of people who seek or find salvation without having ever read *The Geeta*."

Sengupta's writing sweeps all the hypocrisy away while it announces with gusto that Sir, you cannot attain salvation by being a couch- potato. You must work, because you are not entitled to inaction, as urges *The Geeta: na hi kascit ksanam api jatu tisthaty akarma-krt/ karyate hy avasah karma sarvah prakrti-jair gunaih* ["Nobody ever remains without doing actions, even for a moment indeed, because every being who has no free will is made to do action(s) by the qualities born of *Prakrti* (the source of all)"]. For the sake of explication a parallel can be drawn with Thomas' speech in T.S Eliot's *Murder in the Cathedral*: "They know and do not know, what it is to act or suffer./ They know and do not know, that action is suffering/ And suffering is action." Poet and publisher, Dustin Pickering says: "Sengupta valiantly uses Scriptural texts to turn the afterlife upside down." Poet and academic, Mary Madec corroborates and suggests this volume of "Flash Wisdom" shows us "what salvation might mean today."

Sengupta conglomerates this in his writing when he argues in a chapter named "Paradise," that his psoriasis ridden mother, who has given her sweat and blood to the well-being of the family is closer to salvation rather than people who "donate and meditate." These last rhyming words are consciously put together by this angry young writer. I was reminded of one of the verses from his preceding book, *The Earthen Flute* —"*Mantra bears lust ... petty you, you blame the luster!*"

Sengupta aptly captures the essence of the general unthinking mass when he questions the preaching of *The Geeta*: "Never consider yourself to be the cause of the results of your activities, nor be attached to inaction". How appalling would it be if a murderer were to imbibe this? But instead, Sengupta brings into discussion (the action/inaction of) a childless couple, and here is the general broth of wry humor combined with anger which makes the book so unique. In a chapter titled "Bondage," Sengupta dubs every unsuccessful fertilization of the ovum as "link failure." Keeping aside the style, this is a typical argument which was undertaken by Soren Kierkegaard in his *Fear and Trembling*, where he was flabbergasted at the hypothetical situation — what if every father in the nation had thought himself an Abraham and had tried to murder his son (Isaac) in order to gain God's grace? What if they missed the point — the point of "angst" that Abraham suffered, oscillating between human and divine love? Similarly, in Sengupta, what if religion teaches you (with misrepresentations, of course) to take the easy way — of renunciation? Who would teach them that renunciation is never easy, that even the Buddha had to enter the womb of *Mayadevi* (maya? a metaphor for earthly life?) as the Bodhisattva so that he could preach firsthand the meaning of salvation and deliver people? Who would care to tell them that renunciation has to be attained through the path of ultimate desire: "Salvation is but enlightenment, achievable only by actions, and through your sensory gateways?" Salvation, as Sengupta thinks, exists as a posited, non-thetic being, that has nothing to do with renunciation, or only partly so, because, it cannot be fully perceived by our conscious being, because, it is in it, and is not what our conscious cogitates and posits it to be, if we try to explain this by Sartre's theory of being. Sengupta's discourse, here, immediately connects to Lord Krishna's speech in *The Mahabharata*, where he says that the sole purpose of life is self-realization; it is a strife to remind oneself how great one is in the sense that each being (*Jeevatma* — microcosm) is a part of Himself (*Paramatma* — macrocosm). This realization has to be attained through action, through work (categorized into *Sattva*-the ideal kind, *Rajas*-spurious with a tad bit of pride, and *Tamas*-the vilest kind), which would propel an individual towards salvation or damnation. Sengupta does not commit; but vanquishes everything that reeks of superstition.

Let me conclude by referring to the very first chapter in this collection, "Saffron." He writes: "We are perhaps glued to the holy *shaligram*, and we nurture the very thought of listening to the loud chants of the religious verses". The *shaligram* is an anthropomorphic symbol for the *Vaishnavites*—made of a string of beads with four for a set, each bead representing one weapon of the lord—*Sankha* (the conch), *Chakra* (the wheel), *Gada* (the mace), and the *Padma* (the lotus). The idea is the arrangement of these weapons in different ways (factorial of four=24 ways) and one name of the Lord is assigned for each assignment. You can almost feel the giddiness among the chants, going round and round like a carousel and leaving you dizzy headed, and more importantly at the same place. You are made to revel in the verses, and not in what they actually signify— you remain immersed in the imperfect lyrics and deviate from the music which is the true essence of art, which would have led you to the coveted "Oneness" (Friedrich Nietzsche, *The Birth of Tragedy*) with the Almighty, because then you are following the right path and actually know your aim. This is a vivid yet disturbing image that Sengupta produces, and establishes the fact that Sengupta is here to stay— he is not just another writer among the mass.

Reflections on Salvation is highly recommended, for it won't waste your time, your most precious resource. These lines would be the most memorable of the new things you'll read this year: "*We live as long as we breathe; and it is but the breathing which occurs on its own will. No gods, but the breath that builds a home for our life and death. / They say, God dwells within; it is then the mortal exploration of the resort where salvation is largely seen.*" The book won't tell you how to think, but would importantly point out that you need to think. High time!

Reflections on Salvation: A necessary read
Pranab Ghosh

What is the relevance of religious text in modern times? What if one is not devout enough to embrace it with unquestioning submission? To a modern man undergoing the day-to-day grind to survive, religion could be an escape from the stress and strain. S/he may find solace in a place of worship where mantras are chanted. He may look up to God as his path to salvation. But what is salvation? Is it an escape from the worldly cycle of birth and death? And if it is so how does s/he achieve it? Would it be through the process of renunciation?

Kiriti Sengupta through his eighteen short poetic prose pieces in *Reflections on Salvation*, a "collection of anecdotal wisdom that serves to both illuminate and discuss the paradox of faith," as pointed out by Dustin Pickering, the founder of Transcendent Zero Press, [Houston, Texas] in his publisher's note, attempts to answer these questions from a point of view that is neither religious nor scholastic. Sengupta makes it clear in the introductory chapter of the book: "But then, mine is not a scholastic work by any means. I have no intention to start an exclusive lineage of devotees, come on!" *Reflections on Salvation* must be read as "a work of literature, which hopefully stir the age-old notion about sacrifice, renunciation and salvation," as the author himself aptly writes in the same chapter. While the devout or the so-called protectors of the Hindu religion may call the work "misrepresentation of scripture" where the author has failed to grasp the real meaning of *moksha* or salvation, the point that one should note is that the author has been upright enough to go beyond what could be called blind faith and has tried to address the apparent contradictions that religious text presents to modern man. Sengupta in the 14th chapter, "Detachment," questions the relevance of the saying of *The Geeta*: "*Karmany-evadhikars te ma phaleshu kadachana / ma karma-phala-hetur bhur ma te sango stvakarmani* (You have a right to perform your duties, but you are not entitled to the fruits of your actions. Never consider yourself to be the cause of the results of your activities, nor be attached to inaction) for a childless couple plagued by infertility. A devout may thrash the author and accuse him of being frivolous, but can one deny the author his right to put an age-old wisdom in its perspective and question its application in modern times? "Situation changes, but scriptures remain the same. Mundane," laments Sengupta in the concluding lines of the chapter.

The author in this book has dealt with the questions that an inquiring, illumined mind may face as he is forced to follow the rituals as have been practiced in the name of religion down the ages. "Why do we commission a priest to worship the household gods? I wonder if we are not capable enough to perform the action on our own," Sengupta questions. He has the answer to it as well. "We are perhaps glued to the sacred thread, the holy *shaligram*, and we nurture the very thought of listening to the loud chants of the religious verses." Is he denouncing religion or religious practices? Not in the least. What he is drawing our attention to is the fact that we can get rid of accepted practices and yet worship God. We can achieve salvation without the mediation of the saffron-clad *sadhu*. "Divinity might be found in conduct, but not in the codes. Understanding the objective of life, or the purpose of your worldly existence is your first step to reach the gods," Sengupta says in the concluding lines of chapter 4, "Conduct."

As for the saffron-clad *sadhu* the author probes beyond the commonly accepted norm and questions the concept of renunciation as is traditionally understood. "I'm telling you, with saffron comes *sannyas* or renunciation, and with renunciation arrives attachment. Attachment with the world, attachment with domesticity, or may be the gods." (Chapter 1, "Saffron") The observation is apt. Why should one differentiate oneself by the attire he wears to drive home the fact that he is more pious than others and closer to the gods? If someone has completed the process of absolute detachment from the society and all worldly ties, why should s/he fall back on society for survival? "A renunciate abandons the family — the root and the society, but comes back to them to secure living. Is the monk honest enough to be named a *sadhu*?" Sengupta questions in the closing lines of Chapter 12, "Return." The devout may become angry at such 'ungodly' conclusion of the author, but given the history of god-men that we have had in our country, can we deny the probing mind its rightful claim to question the accepted norm? After all, every saint is not a Swami Vivekananda.

Sengupta in *Reflections on Salvation*, while questioning the set principles of faith and its application, has displayed a sense of humor that brings to the fore the irony of devotion. "I'm aware of a few families who give funds to the monks and carefully preserve the receipts of their donation. Donors are proud owners of such receipts as those are useful to claim income-tax-exemption. A formally printed donation receipt in India is but a memoir of section 80G!" (Chapter 12, "Return") Author's probing humor gets displayed once more in Chapter 17, "Instinct," where he playfully finds a scriptural excuse that might get Salman Khan, tried for killing a blackbuck, absolved of all charges. "Killers deserve leniency — I wonder if the court is against the Lord." He is more critical, as his humor unmasks the 'relevance' of age-old religious texts in today's world, "*The Vedas* did not count on malnutrition; they did not even consider environment, let alone poverty." (Chapter 9, "Fire")

As for salvation, Sengupta has a logical approach that might help both the believer and the non-believer. He favors action over inaction. Work for him is, as Swami Vivekananda had pointed out, "worship." "Salvation is but enlightenment, achievable only by actions, and through your sensory gateways." (Chapter 5, "Stagecraft") That it is the man who stands tall in the final count becomes clear when he says, "We live as long as we breathe; and it is but the breathing which occurs on its own will. No gods, but the breath that builds a home for our life and death." (Chapter 18, "Salvation")

The author, in the final count, in spite of the fact that he may incur the wrath of a fanatic Hindu, has done a service to common intelligent readers, who are plagued by the push and pull of faith and struggle inwardly before they could come in terms with the concepts of salvation and renunciation and how these could be related to their daily presence. *Reflections on Salvation* is a necessary read for a questioning mind, who finds it difficult to accept faith as it appears in front of him/her packaged in rituals that are hard to accept.

Redefining the canon — Radical art and craft of Kiriti Sengupta: Brief meditation on his book of prose poems: *Reflections on Salvation*

Sunil Sharma

Kiriti Sengupta, a dental surgeon from Kolkata, is industry-trained to deftly operate by digging deep into nano regions. Probing the rough surfaces in circular manner, inside-outside, in quick seconds within an open mouth, requires patience, observation and skill of a high order. Peeling off the enamel, filling up the cavities and decay in complicated procedures with a pair of nimble hands and few gadgets — is challenging for both the doctor and the patient; for the latter, a bit more, as it involves personal space for the inspection of a foreign body. But the end-result is worth the costly ordeal. You get clarity and relief in an hour or so, reclined on the chair, a soft medium in the expert hands of a person in white; pleased with the state of temp nirvana, post-consultation. The doctor-assisted process is intricate—

Evaluation
Relief from pain
Illumination
[About your disease, from the specialist]

And a regimen to avoid frequent visits and the daunting prospect of getting teeth pulled out or in, with mouth open but gagged. Majority listens to the advice and acts accordingly to avoid an unavoidable repeat performance … or until the time, it can be further postponed.

Kiriti Sengupta is no ordinary surgeon. He is a globally recognized writer, editor, blogger, columnist, interviewer, promoter … and these days, a sage poet dispensing *gyan* [wisdom] to those seeking escape from pain and suffering, but this time, of different scale — caused by/to mind and soul.

Reflections on Salvation [*RoS*] is a handbook of a sort for the hurried. Or, is it a help book? Or, is it a string of pearls that in a bland syntax, literary journalists might opt to call wisdom?

No coincidence that it is your favorite dental surgeon, who is often tasked with the job of extracting that last tooth [third molar] giving a lot of discomfort and some insight/hindsight into the existential suffering inherited in general by human body in an otherwise violent and absurd world of mall-killings, suicide bombers and sectarian cleansing! Wisdom! Wisdom tooth, and the dental surgeon, as your typical angel, is on the call.

No doubt, Marquez dedicated one of his magic-realist short fictions to — whom else, but a dental surgeon in a troubled part of the world. And Marquez devotees love that story.

The same set of cognitive, mental and visual skills combined with dexterity is brought into play by the artist Kiriti in his latest offering, the *RoS*. The scientific, medical, poetic and speculative side of a scholar gets enmeshed in this line of inquiry manifest in the book published in the United States. From evaluation to enlightenment; decay to restoration; pain to relief; inside to outside in a circular motion, and finally, a few of gleaming pearlies that reflect back from the coated surface. In the present context, a series of glittering words that render new insights into the very nature of reading/writing/cognition and praxis. The entire procedure is minimal and non-invasive and leads to heightened clarity.

Reflections on Salvation is a verbal probe into the perplexing duality of the past/present; the dynamics of heritage/contemporaneity; sacred/sacrilege; tradition/modernity; word/meaning; signifier/signified; construct/constructed and de-constructed for another re-construction in an endless play.

Through the book of "random" thoughts, Kiriti undertakes and destabilizes the very act of hermeneutics and sets up the democratic right of the well-informed reader to assert their right and autonomy of their objective reading of a pluralistic text.

In a way, it recalls the bold gesture of Martin Luther or Galileo in resisting the official hierarchies involved in the solitary act of reading texts or interpreting things held sacred by the politics of a given era.

Kiriti is here on a demolition job. Working on a stream of ideas like Joyce but in a different direction, Kiriti questions the authority and weight of opinion accumulated carefully by a Brahiminical system of regulation of thought; a hegemonic structure of policing and power over national imagination and collective perception of reality as evidenced in great texts. He interrogates the rituals, chants, thread, holy books, color code — the entire signifying system of the Hinduism, analyzed in small paragraphs called chapters, in total eighteen.

It is Zen-kind of meditation triggered by insignificant things that lead to most significant insights, views on a hoary past informing our present through a clutch of symbolic practices designed to perpetuate an outdated order of moral authority and sacredness for a priestly class, out of sync with a tech society with its own mythologies.

In simple prose, Kiriti deftly delivers the key results, working on nano spaces and decaying surfaces of our communal existence.

Take this parable called "Third Molar":

> A woman came to my clinic with a carious wisdom tooth. She had severe pain and wanted immediate relief. I made the tooth numb by lignocaine. Once relieved the woman became insistent and said that she wanted to save the affected tooth. I had to decline and prescribed a few medicines that would eliminate inflammation in the first place. I advised her to return after five days and get her tooth removed. She didn't agree and named a few modern

procedures that might help her. She even questioned my skill, "Aren't you aware of atraumatic restorative treatment?"

I could not help it; I smiled and said, "Trauma necessarily precedes wisdom! (page 6)

This is illustrative! A doctor and his mundane world of instruments, light, sedatives and suffering patients in search of instant relief in a well-equipped dental studio; a sharp intellect searching for answers in that clutter and deadening routine, and, finding the perfect answer to the riddles of the complex universe, in a wisdom tooth.

Again, the binary of insignificant/significant gets revered and its arbitrary nature revealed through such an investigation of truth. The conclusion is beautiful: "Trauma necessarily precedes wisdom!"

This is a classic Zen-moment: A Zen epiphany. Call it by any name. The truth is couched as a simple one liner … short … succinct … luminous — like a rain drop, detached from heavens and resting on a blade of grass in a lonely meadow, away from the highway and its machine madness.

Surrounded by the tools of his craft/trade, Kiriti articulates the benefits of pain to a disciple-like figure: Better awareness of the universe is obtained through most unlikely routes, in this case, a molar. Baby Krishna showed the cosmic reality to his mother in his widely opened mouth!

That pain, trauma and death are the springs of religion and philosophy are a well-known fact. Siddartha knows this the most. Operating in that environment, Kiriti ponders over human condition like an adept and comes up with his own manifesto in the form of the illuminating *RoS*. Take another look on color saffron:

> Why do we commission a priest to worship the household gods? I wonder if we are not capable enough to perform the action on our own. We are perhaps glued to the sacred thread, the holy *shaligram*, and we nurture the very thought of listening to the loud chants of the religious verses. Aren't we cursed badly by ourselves?
>
> Saffron adds color and flavor to certain delicacies, but when it shows up on your attire, I find you saintly pious. It is all in my mind that has been grossly tuned to accept and refuse the effects of the colors they carry within. I'm telling you, with saffron comes *sannyas* or renunciation, and with renunciation arrives attachment. Attachment with the world, attachment with domesticity, or may be the gods.
>
> How does one become a monk? Is it by renouncing the fruits of actions one undertakes? Even the gods invite dependence, and remember, they are considered superior to the saints! ("Saffron," page 1)

In this engaging candid conversation with a reader, Kiriti lays out the contours of the map beforehand, in the introductory chapter. Here is the essence of the journey surmised for writer and reader:

The Geeta has been interpreted by many scholars, saints and monks down the ages. One considers another wrong or bad. One interpretation invites another, and it has been observed that what once had been referred to as a right interpretation, has later been criticized as a misinterpretation. Why do we need an interpretation of the verses as contained in *The Geeta*? The verses are meant to be read, absorbed, felt, and followed, and one would need an enlightened Master or Guru to guide followers. Even the Masters differ while explaining the teachings of the scripture, and who am I to utter the final words? I have no intention to start an exclusive lineage of devotees, come on!

Scripture does not allow one to be judgmental. Scriptural verses deserve contemplation, and *Reflections on Salvation* is a work of literature, spread across eighteen short chapters, which hopefully stir the age-old notion about sacrifice, renunciation and salvation. ["Have You Secured a Happy Afterlife?," page iv]

Kiriti's prose is deceptively innocuous, especially the last line that declares that the writing intends to "stir' the age-old notion about sacrifice, renunciation and salvation. It, indeed, does. It stirs the concoction skillfully and serves the stir-fried meal for hungry soul. What is sacred? What is reading? Are the values of the ancient religion, *Santana Dharma*, of *The Geeta* relevant in a materialistic world; a world of consumption and instant gratification, in a global market where every item gets neatly labeled and sold to that segment of interested consumers?

What is the autonomy of an enlightened reader in this packaged and pre-ordered universe? Can rites be re-interpreted? Can such a meditation be called literary? Or, philosophy? Can random thoughts — stream of consciousness carefully manipulated, cultivated, edited, designed and then published in that beckoning capitalist nation U.S.A. be called art or serious writing? Is speculation an art? Philosophy?

Well, to me, here lies Kiriti's genius. He re-defines the boundaries and the canon like every serious artist. He is radical in pushing and reformulating the genre and making us see the Keatsian truth in a Grecian urn, despite the opacity/age, on the strength of his sincerity and conviction and a fluid style. Kiriti Sengupta is avant-garde. He announces a kind of writing inaugurated earlier by Woolf and Joyce that challenges the ossified order, traditional narrative, representational modes and ushers in a new way of seeing/reporting/documenting the falling atoms.

In a way, Kiriti subverts the writing process also and de-centers the old ways of thinking/seeing by heralding New Writing that is enthusiastic, bubbly, ecstatic and questioning the old modes and searching for new answers to some fundamental questions of civilization. Through *RoS*, he attempts a new poetics of existence, human condition, through a restrained lyricism and spiritual debate and produces a revamped episteme about scriptures held dear by a culture and its managers for their own monopoly and survival in a caste society, on the brink of transformation by economic and tech forces. The R*o*S is Baconian in its insistence on knowing the nature of reason and Sartrean for trying to understand the nature of being and choice-freedom in a circumscribed world, over-determined. The book is a new renaissance valorizing the individual and placing that Rousseau-figure over and above tradition and the belief that our inner reason, conscience, is capable of realizing the sacred within: "They say God dwells within!" ("Salvation," page 18)

Human agency: It is an assertion of humanism over the stranglehold of stale custom and hierarchical religion and liturgy.

The style is poetic that is resonant. The descriptions are lucid and brief for a reader on a go. The R*o*S is modern classic that refuses to be pigeonholed and thus, destabilizes the very artificial nature of canon-formation; categorization; labeling of intellectual discourse, its boundaries and taxonomy practices by a culture ready for branding/selling every experience. It is a book for the quester willing to navigate global pathways to new knowledge. The surgeon and artist delivers … a Savant-sage has arrived!

Gopal Lahiri interviewed Kiriti Sengupta

Kiriti Sengupta is an essential and powerful voice of our time. He writes on a gentler sublime potency of life and his clear eyed attention brings each topic into dizzying focus. He makes his writing all that easy yet his wit and analytical mind create an immediacy. Kiriti once remarked, "Poetry is an occasion for rejoicing ... celebrating the earth, birth and exit through the earthen flute. After all, poets are not beggars, but seekers of the truth." This sums up all.

Gopal Lahiri: You are a versatile writer and already authored nine books at such a young age. What started you writing poetry, non-fiction or memoir? Which one you like most?

Kiriti Sengupta: Thank you! I'll turn forty-two on April 29 this year. I've grey hair ... my skin shows signs of aging; I'm an old soul, you see! You were right when you said I've authored nine books, but then, I've two full-length collections of translated poems as well. My life — experiences I gain on a day-to-day basis and, the observations that either support or challenge my experiences — they inspire me to write. Be it poetry, nonfiction or memoir, the life has been the great teacher and I'm one of its unruly students. I'm particularly fond of free verse; do you know why? It allows me to challenge a set of rules which often restrict the flow of my creative juices.

Lahiri: Are there any themes which particularly attract you as a writer?

Sengupta: Water attracts me more than the mountains! Water symbolizes life. When you feel restless look at the water, they say. It calms your mind. Poetry crystallizes best in tranquility. Poetry is one unique stress-buster available to mankind.

Lahiri: Tell us about yourself, your profession, your spirituality and of course about your readers?

Sengupta: I believe I'm a reliable dental surgeon to my patients. My only son, Aishikk, rarely finds me in the house as I mostly stay away due to my work. Trust me, my wife, Bhaswati, has no complaint, and I'm grateful to her for allowing me the needed space to pamper my pen! I'm planning to buy a studio where people can read their favorite books while munching cheese sandwiches. You know, cheese and smile are inter-related for ages. I can assess and design smiles from being a trained cosmetic dentist. I've a few dedicated readers; they are my strength.

Lahiri: Who are our favorite authors?

Sengupta: A long list that starts with Tagore; I consider myself a big fan of Wordsworth. I love to read Sharmila Ray, Sunil Sharma, Sanjeev Sethi, Ananya S Guha, Atreya

Sarma Uppaluri, Chandra Shekhar Dubey, among others. Seshu Chamarty's Haikus are astounding. Did I name you? I'm a proud owner of *Living Inside*, which is your book. Of late Raghavendra Madhu's debut book, *Make Me Some Love to Eat*, has been a great reading experience! Among young American poets I'll name Dustin Pickering and Scott Thomas Outlar.

Lahiri: Tell us about the writers who have influenced you.

Sengupta: Don Martin [Arizona, USA] has hugely influenced my writing style. It's his ease of expression that made me a conscious writer. And then, Vibha Malhotra. Vibha is a perfectionist. I think she can immaculately reciprocate her mind whenever she writes. This is a commendable take. I can tell you Vibha is very particular about punctuation — all in all, an enviable creative writer!

Lahiri: You are an accomplished poet and clarity is the hallmark of your writing. How do you approach poetry?

Sengupta: When you say 'clarity' I remember the poem, "Clarity," I wrote a few years ago. Clarity is like making clarified butter (*ghee*) from milk. You boil milk for hours, let it cool and separate the yellow froth that forms on its surface. You accumulate the froth in a container and boil it to produce fresh and pure *ghee*. Achieving clarity in writing asks for simple living. Accepting life as it arrives and how quickly one absorbs the challenges to survive — you live in several productive ways, yet remain free of ambitions ... the entire theory may sound interesting, however it is difficult to follow and attain. But, as soon as you secure patience and simplicity, you will certainly show distinct signs of clarity in your work. My poems elicit the facets of my philosophy, especially the life I chose to live.

Lahiri: In your last book *Reflections on Salvation*, you mentioned, "Scripture does not allow one to be judgmental. Scriptural verses deserve contemplation." Can you elaborate to the tune of the context of the book?

Sengupta: One of the chief objectives of studying the scriptures is to live a restrained and disciplined life. Scriptural studies can make you a *pundit*, scholar and, even a knowledgeable human, but you will require 'practice' to become a truly wise being. Real wisdom opens one's heart and makes one earthy, compassionate and generous. Scriptures should make men sensible. You see, the scriptures have been written in verses which often mask the real meaning of them. Exploring them through austere practice is called for. There are several commentaries available on the scriptures, but they create confusion and the commentators should be held responsible if the resultant confusion generates division and lack of integrity in mankind. *The Gita* says: *sarvadharman parityajya/ mam ekam saranam vraja* (chapter 18, verse 66). If we go by its literal translation, we have been advised to abandon all varieties of religion and surrender ourselves unto the God. The same verse has been explained in more than one way in the commentaries, and one must keep a note of the fact that the so-called religions like Hinduism, Islam,

Christianity, etc. were not in existence during the making of *The Gita* which essentially belongs to the *Sanatana Dharma* (Eternal Religion). I'll say it again, "Scriptural verses deserve contemplation!"

Lahiri: Once you said, "I believe when life can be random, why would I possibly plan to order and smoothen the transitions? Let them remain as-it-is." Do you think that this is an essential gradient of good writing?

Sengupta: Life is random, you see! You come across numerous transitions which are utterly rough, unexpected and disturbing. You don't have an option to decline them; you have to traverse the avenues that life has planned for you. You have no choice, but to face the seemingly unpleasant obstacles. You stumble upon, and then decide to walk further. Your muscles absorb the shock and adjust themselves to receive more. The brain instructs you to be careful in future. Similarly, if you "plan to order and smoothen the transitions" from one chapter of your writing to another, you would perhaps fail to stir the minds of your readers. A good write should hit and boggle the mind.

Lahiri: Share your learning experiences from being an editor, publisher and also a critic as well.

Sengupta: I'm still learning from being an editor. As publisher I've released several important titles over the last few years. I often ask the young authors, "Why would one buy your book? I can understand that your friends and family will buy your book; they can appreciate and even critique your work. But, how would you reach out to someone whom you don't know at all?" The authors try to explain, but lack reasoning. I've seen many young talents dream of being successful and sought-after overnight with the release of their debut books, irrespective of the genre they prefer to write. My work schedule rarely allows me to write reviews of books, but then, I do write a review or two as and when I read something that taps my mind.

Lahiri: You are an accomplished translator. If I put it that way, on which side does your weight fall, the translator or a writer of your own?

Sengupta: Writers (be poet/ novelist/ nonfiction writer/ essayist) are essentially translators of their thoughts. But translating others' lines of thought is extremely tedious and exhaustive. But then, I love to be marked as the translator of a few celebrated Bengali poets whom I look up to. At all events I'll prefer to be remembered as a writer or poet in connection with the books I've authored.

Dustin Pickering interviewed Kiriti Sengupta

Kiriti Sengupta is author of *The Freshman's Welcome*; the bestselling trilogy: *My Glass of Wine*, *The Reverse Tree*, and *Healing Waters Floating Lamps*; and recently, *The Earthen Flute*. *The Earthen Flute* is a bestselling collection in both India and America in Indian literature. Sengupta works in Calcutta in dentistry and likes to nurture friendships with younger writers. I caught him in a moment of contemplation after his newest book hit the shelves.

What inspires you the most to continue writing?

My studies, observations and living! If you want me to elaborate on them, it will take pages, but I would like to state that I study to observe, and I observe to reflect on my studies. I am no way close to what you say as "ideal living," and I truly look out for holistic living measures. You know, we often talk about "evidence-based-dentistry," and my life essentially complies with living evidences. Honestly, it is the deviation from the set-rules that keeps me going.

Do you set aside a time for writing? Is there a moment in your daily activities when you feel most inspired?

Nothing like that. My friends consider me happy-go-lucky kind of a guy! People often say, "You don't look like a writer, let alone a poet." I appreciate their views, and unless I feel like pouring out my words I don't write even an update on Facebook. I don't enjoy a set time that I can devote to my writing. I am a practicing dental surgeon, I manage a small press as well. I meet authors and poets on and off. And yes, I don't socialize as it is expected from a family person. I don't write on a daily basis, but my mind quickly registers the observations, which let me thrive on them.

What is your daily life like? Does it get entwined with your poetry?

I have a day job, Dustin. As I said before I practice as a dental surgeon, and there are but a few occasions when poetry occurs. Do you remember the poem "Envy" in my latest collection, *The Earthen Flute*? It's got humor, it also bore sarcasm. Above all, "Envy" could be treated as psychosomatic poetry, but readers might consider it weird. Listen to these lines, and I hope you won't mind:

Jealous—
A Dentist can say if you are one

Your teeth deviate from
The occlusal table
And thus, lips suffer from bites

Is there a place for poetry and literature in India's popular imagination? It seems Americans find it dull and tedious.

Poetry is popular only among poets, worldwide! One who appreciates poetry writes poetry. He/she may not be a published poet, but then you need not to write a poem on a paper, or on your cellphone to establish your claim of being a poet. What name would you like to offer to someone who continues to write poetry in his/her mind? There are numerous such people, and they hardly wish to be marked as poet. I'll love to call them "non-practicing poets." And poetry essentially thrives on both the practicing and non-practicing group of poets.

India is considered the spiritual capital of the world. We had innumerable sages and monks who made verses popular in our land. And then, we had Tagore, who made global readers serious about Bengali poetry. Poetry is an extremely important ingredient of Indian culture and philosophy. The corporate India may not be interested in literature or poetry, but they don't govern our heritage in any capacity.

In America, we host "slams": poetry competitions based on performance. This seems to be the most popular outlet for poetry's expression. Does India have a specific outlet poetry finds itself in?

Honestly, I am not aware of poetry competitions in India. We have a few important literary festivals that happen annually, but I don't think they dedicate even half of their tenure to poetry. Probably in all major cities we have groups of poets, but then I wonder, if they are, in any way, instrumental in bringing out quality poetry.

Tell me about your upcoming collection. Is there a message you wish to convey? Who are you addressing your words to?

My newest book of poems is titled *The Earthen Flute*. Kolkata based Hawakaal Publisher has published and launched it formally on Feb 21 (2016) in Calcutta. My poetry essentially bears messages that I wish to convey to my readers. But I am not the right person to state those messages, for poetry is reader-specific. There are twenty-one poems in this book; short, long, and prose-poems. A few of them have appeared in literary journals and blogs. I have added fresh poems as well. There are illustrations that add to the appeal. All in all, *The Earthen Flute*, I'm pretty sure, is going to be a collector's edition. Truth-seekers and poetry lovers around the world may find my work worthy! You will be glad to know that my book has been reviewed on *The Lake* magazine (United Kingdom) even before its release. You may read the complete preview on this link: http://www.thelakepoetry.co.uk/reviews/february16/

The *Millennium Post* (English daily published both in Calcutta and New Delhi) said:

> In this collection of 21 poems, Sengupta talks about how the modern youth is obsessed by what is trendy but ignorant about the wisdom that ancient mythology is laden with. "For example, in a poem titled "Cryptic Idioms," I talk

about how we follow certain yogic postures without even realizing that these were actually part of Sanatan Dharma or Hindu mythology," Sengupta told *Millennium Post*.

Do you feel your poetry is more personal or transcendent? If personal, how does the average reader relate? If transcendent, how do you reach that state?

If my poetry is personal or transcendent, critics can answer this best. I don't write poetry to make it personal or the other way round. I try to convey messages. Some call them "wisdom messages," others may term my poetry surrealistic! I'm not bothered, you see. I remain conscious when I compose a poem, but poetry essentially arrives without a notice. Let me quote a few lines from a critique:

> If Sengupta were to follow T.S. Eliot's dictum that true art should be impersonal, what would that lead to? The clash of opinions still persists — that between the romantic school and the modernist school — Sengupta adheres to the romantic school of thought. It's the creator's choice and I guess it's right for him because if he were to turn impersonal, that would take away the essence of his signature poems, the unique subjective and personal

elements. (Page 33, Ketaki Datta and Tania Chakravertty/*Rhapsodies and Musings*/ Hawakaal Publishers/ July 2015)

I can remember a commentary on my trilogy:

Worldly observations become the occasion for explorations of meanings: of the self and its status within the world and within consciousness, and of life's journey from birth to death ... While Sengupta's poems touch the spirit, and often deal with spiritual matters, they are uniformly grounded in the world around us. (Casey Dorman/ *The Statesman*/ Jan 31, 2016)

What characterizes a good poet from a bad one? Are there objective criteria? Can habit make a person a poet? What distinguishes a poet from one who writes poetry?

These are difficult to answer, Dustin! You have added so many brief questions together. Who is a poet, if I may ask? One may be a famous poet, a popular poet, an esteemed poet, an unknown poet, a non-practicing poet, but they all are poets in the first place. They are neither good, nor are they bad. You love a poet, but then do you love all his/her poems? I mean, all poems that he/she writes? You read a not-so-good poem, written by your beloved poet; how would you rate/grade the poet now? When can a writer claim him/her-self as a poet? I never claim myself as a poet. I write poetry, and if I can be named "poet" is to be ascertained by my readers and reviewers. Don't go by the dictionary and name a writer "poet" if he/she writes poetry.

How do you find the time to write?

How do you manage time to eat, Dustin? Aren't you too occupied to manage even a nap? You are to eat and sleep and write. And I am no exception. Hey, did I answer your question?

Do you think the "Muse" is a real being? What purpose does she serve? Who is she? Why does she latch onto certain people?

Do you think the "Muse" is a female being? Why do you think so? The "Muse" is only you, if you understand my point. Let me quote a few lines from *The Earthen Flute*.

> *I'm not a pervert, take a note!*
> *I'm a woman as long as I'm dynamic*
> *I'm a woman unless I'm stilled*
> *Do you think of a woman's voyage to the heaven?* ("Seventh Heaven")

The "Muse" is only your kinetic mind. Your soul keeps wandering to understand the reason(s) of being restless over the years. And it is the "Muse" that allows one to pen down the thoughts of restlessness. You cannot appreciate quietude by keeping mum. You would not be able to celebrate silence if you remain soundless. You have to cultivate the skill of becoming still. Tranquility has its charm when enjoyed in noise. A poet is the blessed soul who struggles for silence and peace, and thus guiding the society in a subtle way towards a harmonious cohabitation with the "Muse."

Do you read a lot? Does reading factor into your writing? What role does reading play for a writer? How much do you read on average?

I'm an average reader. Thanks to my lazy eyes that have made me one such. Long poems tire me, extremely long essays exhaust my brain to no end, and fat novels are too repulsive to sit on my desk. Reading influences the psyche, and thus your writing shows the signs of your reading habit. They say it is important to learn, and even more important to unlearn things.

Do you ever face adversity for being a writer? Are you humiliated or have you been unfairly criticized?

I have my share of negative reviews of my work, but then who I am to justify! I have never paid my reviewers, neither did I influence them in any way. Dustin, why don't you tell the world about how I managed the notes of appreciation (blurbs) from a few American poets in relation with *The Earthen Flute*? I was fairly surprised when both Jonathan Moody and Lorna Dee Cervantes wrote on my work, entirely based on the merit or quality of the manuscript.

I was bullied in school at times for being bookish and was considered a teacher's pet, and sometimes teachers themselves thought I was weird. I never fit in to the in-crowd. Years ago, I had a neighbor who believed people who read were ugly and stupid. He insisted that on his trips to the library, he saw only old people or ugly women. It was extremely

insulting, but I practiced my usual "Christian forbearance" and was kind until he was evicted from the apartment complex for assaulting me (after a long series of mishaps, the manager was tired of him as well). I think with a head of tough wisdom (not the earthly kind, but philosophical like Ecclesiastes) you are bound to writhe some days. I haven't had harsh critiques from publishers or reviewers, and most other poets have a favorable attitude toward my writing. This has been a lifelong pursuit for me, beginning when I wrote a short story called *The Little Red Wagon*, written from a child's imagination. The story was about a young man who loses a wheel off his wagon, and searches for it all day only to find it at the day's end where he least expects it. I developed a strong sense of the calling at a young age, taking advice from my grandmother on both reading habits and approaches to writing. In your opinion, what is the greatest thing to be proud of as a poet?

Honestly, I have no idea. You know, I once asked Bibhas Roy Chowdhury why a poet feels insulted when he/she is referred to as writer. He told me, "Poet is the highest adjective available to a writer."

What other writers you admire? Who is currently on your "to read" list?

I have a long list that starts with Tagore and ends with you, Dustin. I would prefer not to take their names, for they are admired on the basis of their poetry. I'm now reading two books: *When God Is A Traveller* by Arundhathi Subramaniam, and *The Daunting Ephemeral.*

Does writing serve a purpose for non-writers? Comedian Jerry Seinfeld once said the secret to his success was writing every day. How do you think writing can help those who aren't writers?

Ask a psychotherapist and you will understand how writing helps an individual in his/her day-to-day life. Writing helps in more than one way to combat stress, depression and mental blockage. I must tell you, Dustin, I used to write uncountable love-letters to my girl-friend who is now my wife.

What is literacy like in India? What type of literature does the average Indian read?

India is no exception, we love to value fiction stories more than any other genre of literature.

Finally, is there still a sense of the sacred in India where much of the sacred was born?

India is a holy land; the land of spirituality. Even now we have a handful of realized souls, and I am proud to have been associated with a few of those Masters.

My Husband-turned-Writer
Kiriti Sengupta
Bhaswati Sengupta

Kiriti's desire to become a writer was unwelcome, as far as I was concerned. When he first ventured into writing, and simultaneously we were being bogged down with problems connected with the family coupled with an enocomic crisis as well, I was kind of apathetic if not sort of irritated with his choice... Maybe more so because of poetry, it would have been different if it was prose, because poetry had never been that close to my soul. Even then, after so many years, I might as well confess, although I take pride in his works, I find the emotional surplus that should have been there, missing in its place.

I do not have any friend, at the moment there is no one in this planet whom I can call a friend; whom I can share my apprehensions or discomforts with; but to speak the truth, I do not repent much, as I always have two new books waiting for me, alongside my own hard-earned money. And for that, I do not have to think much before buying a new book. This is the natural bent due to which I should have been more involved with Kiriti's books. It did not happen that way.

The reason for this might be that while Kiriti had been busy with his works, I had been walking down a parallel path, the stumbles on which have mitigated or have completely done with certain emotions in me. Further, I had my doubts. What Kiriti had been writing, has he been totally integrated with it? For he has his faults in him still intact. Even now Kiriti is easily irritable; Even now Kiriti hurls inappropriacies at people when he is angry with them; so how is it that he has evolved? And if he has not, then what is the source behind the imprint of his writing? But evolved he had, or else how could he write? His knowledge of literature was not exhaustive. Even his reading of Shakespeare or Tagore wasn't extensive. Somewhere there is a divine intervention behind this, but is Kiriti *justified* with it? These questions have always struck me while I have seen Kiriti grow as a poet. Although I do not crave an answer. I want to experience his journey alongside him and understand the why or when of the resolution of this doubt.

[Translated from its original Bengali by Koushik Sen]

My beloved Kiriti*da*
Munshi Md.Younus

Debapriya*da*, one of my senior friends from Jadavpur University, introduced me to Dr. Kiriti Sengupta on a social media site. He told me that Dr. Sengupta has authored a poetry collection titled *Reflections on Salvation*. He added that the same has been translated (creatively rewritten) into Bangla and Sanskrit. And the publishers have arranged a book launch event in Oxford Bookstore in New Delhi. Debapriya*da* requested me to speak on the Bangla work. I readily agreed to the offer. Firstly because, a *Jadavpurian* [one who has been taught in Jadavpur University] hardly refuses a request made by another *Jadavpurian*. And secondly, I thought it would be fun to be a speaker in the event. As soon as I agreed Dr. Sengupta phoned me. It was a formal call; honestly, I felt different. Before the formal event Dr. Sengupta and I spoke mostly about the book, and those conversations made him familiar to me.

Finally, we meet in Oxford Bookstore as scheduled. We hugged as we saw one another for the first time. Truly speaking, I felt like receiving an older brother in my life — one who wears a genuine smile. So pure! So generous!

And thus, our story began. We are friends, like brothers; moreover, we think we share the blessings of the Great Soul. I know very little of Dr. Sengupta, except for his physical appearance, and a few facts like he has authored ten books of his own, he is married and his only son is now studying in the seventh grade, and also, Dr. Sengupta owns a publishing press, Shambhabi, that has released my first collection of Bangla poems of late!

But, are those facts really important? I think it is indeed relevant to learn Dr. Sengupta as a human being. I fondly call him Kiriti*da* and he is a true friend. He values commitments and stands by his friends at all events.

Do I write more? Men like Kiriti*da* are a rarity these days and I'll wish him good luck in all his future endeavors.

A Letter to Kiriti Sengupta
Bitan Chakraborty

Dear Kiriti*da,*

It came to pass that the revered editor has commended even me to write about you. What do I write about you? Kiriti*da* the person or Kiriti*da* as a writer? What do I write about a person whom I know for two years? Does the veneer dissipate in two years' time? No, it doesn't. And why should it? If it does, the enigma that makes up every turn of life would have been missed. Why would it be that life stops surprising us? Being familiar with a writer is much easier in two years, for it is difficult to hide behind words, at any rate to an conscious reader. So it's better to talk about writing. Now you'd say, "So, a letter! This was not *my* order!" Agreed, it was not, you have been the harbinger, but I guess this should be directly addressed to you, for it is not often that a reader can open up to the author in this manner, without inhibition.

Let me start with a Spiderman-like approach, skipping your earlier works and talking about *Reflections on*

Salvation. This is because I have been a witness to the writing process of the same. And because, I tried to translate it into Bangla. No, I won't be pedantic or brag about myself if that's what you worry about. Some days ago, I heard a scholar say that you have shown the courage to go back to religion in a time when everyone is so piqued by it (not to say religion fuelled terrorism). Now, I couldn't quite make out the meaning of such a sentence owing to my ignorance. I have been in awe since. An array of questions have pricked my mind, for instance, is it then best not to return to our roots? Does religion mean just the rituals, or why is atheism in vogue, or have we not drawn enough from our true religion? Actually, I do not want to call this *religion*. This is an alliance, of mind and reflection! We attain this alliance. And maybe you call the prayer for attaining this alliance, religion. And this prayer is not a single entity, is has with it embalmed our desire, lust and greed. Actually greed. The greed to acquire the entire planet. I am not speaking of acquiring anything within us. This sense of possession gives us the taste of power. And those things that we own within provides us with an inner strength. That is why this tussle never retreats. Why would it stop? Greed is on the prowl every moment to grab and possess, while this inner strength says with a chuckle, "I will get it just like that. I don't have to extend my hands towards it or flex my muscles for it." Then, greed is bound to crack, being parched out of its strength. This is why *Reflections on Salvation*. Questions between the levels of questions, and questions to one's self. Yes, I affirm consistently that these questions were aimed at your "self," and readers are here but faraway stars. This book is an attempt to open up one's self and rediscover oneself on every level, there is nothing against religion here. When you come across every word of this book, you should be reminded of who you are and your purpose on earth. In these turbulent times, being able to be composed *is* prayer. No, the work does not end in calming oneself. Our mission is to keep our comforting palms on every heated, tormented heart and being able to say, "Return to consciousness. God's wailing won't stop until you are calm." Alas, saying this is easy, and easier said than done. Leave the doing part to the saints. Our part ends at saying. Responsibilities over. But then why have we chosen to write? Why have we chosen to paint on this gigantic canvas? For praises? Or is this another game of power equations? Kiriti*da*, will we too, walk on the same path? Raise slogans like 'Life has its own course' and 'Art is sublime' and while away our days? The flowers for our worship are the words we establish, thinking is our prayer, and even you say, we should not ask for all the good stuff from God, or else where will all the evil go? We can aspire to be the *Neelkantha*, the poison drinker *Shiva*, or else where will we find Him? If we fill the altar with greed, where will be the space for Him?

Look, how I have digressed! I was to talk about your works, but the principles of a blabberer! His disposition always takes him on wayward courses, and only boxing his ears puts him on a straight track. Let's return to your work. I still remember how I was on the last page of *Reflections*, the road leaving me behind, much like the retreat of a tapestry, in that spirit—"They say God dwells within; it is the mortal exploration of the resort where salvation is largely seen!" I was thinking, how to express this in my own words! No, then there was no ides that I will translate your work. I needed to know the meaning, in my own way, in my own language. "God lives within me". This is to happen, predestined. So then does salvation lie in our ability to find Him in ourselves? No, why this alone, for He dwells everywhere, so the process of being able to able to be united with Him is *salvation* for me. Like brick by brick the mason reaches the peak of the temple, likewise, we need to be tangled within the very quotidian-ness of our life is the process to reach Him, this simple statement is the essence of the book! We need to speak these simple things in these troubled times. When sheer madness and and intolerance is blocking the door, right then, to be able to break free from all fetters with one, simple but firm push, that *is* salvation. This is my culture. Easy, simple, firm. I have heard that Tagore had been impressed by a Srilankan dance form, and had included it in his dance-drama *Chandalika*. But while adapting it, he suppressed the impetuousness of the original dance and impressed upon the more tranquil side of it. Actually, madness takes us to that level of lunacy where the windows to our soul are closed, darkness thickens, and brings to life the savage cry of the prehistoric life. When even one's child becomes a piece of meat to be consumed.

Kiriti*da*, come let us pray to our God for the light that would flow through those windows. To be united takes up painstaking dedication. It takes up effort to crack open a door that has been closed for so long. But it must be done, for *salvation* is at stake. And you know well, being a father, what a lie one's own salvation is!

Faithfully yours,

Bitan
17 April, 2017
Nimta, Kolkata

[Translated from its original Bengali by Koushik Sen]

The Author is Redundant!

Kiriti Sengupta

I speak when I write prose; and I read when I write poems! This is how I'll love to summarize my take on the books I have authored. Didn't I speak enough when I wrote text on autobiography and nonfiction? Trust me, I don't have Xerostomia, but my mouth has gone dry as I wrote poems. In all my books, I spoke either with myself or with the reader. And under no circumstances I'll offer an explanation to the lines I wrote. You take them; I'm happy. And if you refuse to read, I may feel downcast but only temporarily, you must note. Do you think I'm being rude to my admirers?

During these years I am fortunate to have found more than a handful of readers who took interest in my literary tour and read the books at every possible layover; but, they never bothered to ask for an explanation or two. They were the readers who dared to build images from interpreting my lines as they deem fit. They were the ones who rewrote my books. Readers are mostly introverted and rewrite the books they cherish in their subconscious minds. Did I make a statement here? Come on, I aired my views on my rosy readers.

My books have fetched several commentaries from their critics; varied interpretations of the verses I wrote. Being the writer I have wondered sometime: Did I really mean what the critic wrote about the poem? But then, this calls for a celebration. I celebrate in quietude. I now prefer to keep silent. What's the point in being lavish about the appreciations I have received? They have surfaced on Google; I cannot be held responsible if the search engine brings more than a dozen of results with my name in them. Silence is perhaps the best way to establish the author's conviction to his/her works.

Sometime in 2014 my three books were launched formally in Crossword, Calcutta: *The Unheard I*, *The Reciting Pens* and *My Glass of Wine*. I got three speakers [critics-turned speakers] who spoke on them, and I can remember one of the speakers read a poem titled "Stay Away" from *My Glass of Wine*. The speaker asked if the poem bore personal anecdotes. My answer was brief: "I would rather pass it this time."

Until today I saw several formal launches of my books across India. Every time I remained apprehensive; on such occasions I deliberately prayed to the gods around: Don't let the speaker ask me to explain my verses. I still keep praying to them, for they are available in plenty in my country.

Over the years I have dreamt about a book launch event where the critic-turned-speaker would probe my psyche, tone of delivery, study the probable links they might find associated with my writings and then return to my work for better cognizance. I'll appreciate more if the critic carefully navigates and speaks on the inevitability of the words I chose in a particular poem. Alas! I'm yet to see such a dream event.

On the contrary I've witnessed a few events where the authors happily explained their stand; they went to great lengths to describe their generous contributions to literature; they even theorized their writings being teachers of English literature. During those events I firmly resisted myself from asking the authors: Why are you speaking the lines your critics are expected to say? I failed to ask... You might say I lacked courage. But then, being courteous has nothing to do with being craven.

I can speak endlessly on "politics of publishing," "politics of editing," and "politics of translation" rather than theorizing my works ... rather than describing the influences of my books on literature. Being the author of more than nine books, sole translator of two full-length collections of translated Bengali poems, and co-editor of five literary anthologies I'm in a better position to speak on the aforementioned subjects in the events that may even mark a formal launch of my book.

There are several ways to address a literary work — a book. I will suggest starting right from the front cover page; it may carry a painting, illustration, or photograph. They may act as a gateway to the book and offer valuable insights. I think by avoiding the foreword (if any) or introductory note a reader does not become smart in any way. Forewords by guest authors are actually critiques written essentially in a positive thread. They often help readers as well as critics to work on the book further. Introspection goes a long way to get into the soul of a work. Introspection!

I'm blessed to have received a handful to critics who took time to reflect on my work. Time!

Time is precious and it may refuse to pay everytime one reads and speaks on a book, and critics are essentially readers who must show the world how uniquely they have read and explored a work. Here authors are redundant. I can remember while interviewing Bibhas Roy Chowdhury, renowned Bengali poet, I asked him if he felt heartbroken from being neglected by the media. Bibhas was quick to answer: "[A] poet has to become private with his/her own writings after a certain point of time." Ref: *Word Riot*.

Silence often speaks more than a thousand spoken words. Authors are not bound to explain their work and they enjoy every right to accept or decline the critiques they may receive. Similarly, critics (who are not paid either by the publisher or author) should feel free to reflect on the works they choose for critiquing, and thus, not remaining under any obligation to please anybody under the sun. Honesty pays, and modern literature benefits from the authors who value reticence.

Notes

1. Page 16 — The article was first published on Duane's PoeTree [duanespoetree.blogspot.in]

2. Page 20 — The article was first published on *The Thumb Print* magazine on October 22, 2016.

3. Page 33 — The article was first published on *The Tuck* magazine on October 20, 2016.

4. Page 59 — The article was first published on *The Tuck* magazine on October 13, 2016.

5. Page 70 — The article was first published in *The Statesman* on January 31, 2016.

6. Page 74 — The article was first published on the *Lost Coast Review* [Vol. 7 No. 2, Winter 2016].

7. Page 79 — The article was first published on the *Literary Yard* on April 8, 2017.

8. Page 90 — The article was first published on the *Muse India* [May-June, 2017].

9. Page 97 — The article was first published in the *Harbinger Asylum* [Spring 2016].

10. Page 108 — The article was first published on the *Muse India* [Sept-October 2013]

11. Page 116 — The article was first published in the *Contemporary Vibes*.

12. Page 125 — The article was first published in *The Hans India* on November 10, 2013.

13. Page 130 — The article was first published on Amazon dot com on December 2, 2013.

14. Page 134 — The article was first published on Amazon dot com on September 8, 2014.

15. Page 138 — The article was first published on *The Fox Chase Review and Reading Series* on August 30, 2014.

16. Page 143 — The article was first published on the *Muse India* [Issue 56, 2014].

17. Page 148 — The article was first published on Boloji dot com on January 16, 2014.

18. Page 151 — The article was first published on the *Muse India* [May-June 2015].

19. Page 156 — The article was first published on the *Word Riot* on January 15, 2015.

20. Page 161 — The article was first published in the *Indian Journal of Comparative Literature and Translation Studies* [April, 2015].

21. Page 170 — The article was first published in the *Reviews* [November, 2014].

22. Page 174 — The article was first published on the *Red Fez* magazine [Issue 73, November, 2014].

23. Page 184 — The article was first published on the *Red Fez* magazine [Issue 83, October 2015].

24. Page 188 — The article was first published on the *Lost Coast Review* [Vol. 7 No. 1, Fall 2015].

25. Page 192 — The article was first published on *Literature Studio* on July 13, 2015.

26. Page 195 — The article was first published on the *Red Fez* magazine [Issue 91, July 2016]

27. Page 200 — The article was first published on *The Lake* [February 2016].

28. Page 203 — The article was first published on *The Luxembourg Review* on March 29, 2016.

29. Page 207 — The article was first published on the *Yellow Chair Review* on May 17, 2016.

30. Page 211 — The article was first published on *The Blue Mountain Review* Issue 6, 2017.

31. Page 231 — The article was first published on *Setu*, a bilingual, online magazine, in February, 2017.

32. Page 246 — The article was first published on the *Yellow Chair Review* on September 9, 2016.

33. Page 251 — The article was first published on *The Thumb Print* magazine on September 8, 2016.

34. Page 256 — The article was first published in the *Harbinger Asylum* [Fall 2016].

35. Page 265 — The interview was first published on the *Setu* magazine [March, 2017].

36. Page 271 — The interview was first published in *The Statesman* on March 6, 2016.

37. Page 290 — The article was first published on the *HuffPost* (US edition) on April 26, 2017.

Biographies

Ananya S Guha has been born and brought up in Shillong, North East India. He has seven collections of poetry and his poems have been published worldwide. They have also been featured in several anthologies. He is also a columnist, critic and editor. He now is a Regional Director at the Indira Gandhi National Open University. He holds a doctoral degree on the novels of William Golding.

Atreya Sarma Uppaluri, from Hyderabad, is a poet, freelance editor, writer and translator with eighteen years of experience, he has over seven hundred writings (poems, articles, editorials, reviews, forewords, translations) to his credit. Currently, he is Chief Editor of the *Muse India*. Also its Contributing Editor (Telugu Literature), he has so far presented 4 exhaustive features on Telugu Literature in Muse India. Occasionally, he writes in Telugu as well. Apart from his poetry collection '*Sunny Rain-n-Snow*,' he has edited/translated/ collaborated on eleven books. He has been, since 2013, featuring and encouraging poets through a weekly column "Wordsmith" in *The Hans India*, a Hyderabad based English daily. He is also the official critic of *Metverse*

Muse, an international journal of metrical poetry, published in Visakhapatnam.

Bhaswati Sengupta is a professionally qualified software engineer having passed M.E. from Jadavpur University, Calcutta. She is currently a home maker and takes pride in bringing up her son, Aishikk.

Bishnupada Ray is an Associate Professor of English at the University of North Bengal, West Bengal, India. His poetry has appeared in *Indian Literature, New Quest, Makata, A Hudson View Poetry Digest, Shabdaguchha* and *Revival*. He won a Pushcart Prize nomination in 2009. His latest book of poetry, *Fox Land and Selected Poems*, was published by the Brown Critique in 2016.

Bitan Chakraborty is a well-known Bengali story writer; author of three books of prose and poetry. His much appreciated *Santiram-er Cha* has fetched critical appreciations both in India and abroad.

Casey Dorman grew up in Vancouver, Washington and was educated at the University of Washington in Seattle, Washington, USA, where he majored in psychology and obtained a BS (1965), MS (1967), and Ph.D. (1970). His specialty was neuro-psychology, specifically brain injury and learning disabilities in children. As a clinician he worked in a children's clinic affiliated with Stanford University, and for the Massachusetts Department of Public Health. In 1988 he began teaching at United States International University in San Diego, California. He published over two dozen research articles on child neuro-psychology and co-authored a book, *Cognitive*

Effects of Early Brain Injury, a volume in the *Johns Hopkins Series on Psychiatry and Neuroscience*. After becoming Dean of the School of Human Behavior, he left teaching to direct the mental health training programs for the County of Orange, California, a position from which he retired in 2010. Casey's literary career began in 2004 with the publication of his thriller novel, *I, Carlos* (Seven Locks Press), followed by another thriller, *Pink Carnation* (Publish America) and then four more novels, *Chasing Tales, Where Have All the Young Men Gone? Unquity, Prisoner's Dilemma: The Deadliest Game*, and *Appointment in Mykonos*, published by his own imprint, Avignon Press. In 2009 he began publishing *Lost Coast Review*, a quarterly literary review, which is now in its seventh year. He has two children and five grandchildren and is married to Lai, with whom he lives in Newport Beach, California.

Scuttling past his long teaching and administrative career with random literary creations, **Dalip K. Khetarpal** took up creative writing full-fledged after his retirement. His earlier poems were psychological in nature and dealt basically with the unconscious and subconscious human mind. His first anthology entitled, 'Fathoming Infinity' (Prefaced by Maria Miraglia, Italy) testify to this. But he later shifted his focus to other wider desultory areas of life, like mysterious and complex aspects of man-woman relationship, sex, deceptive myths, mysteries of life, human soul and God with some trace of humanism and sometimes, metaphysicism as reflected in his anthologies titled, 'Ripping into consciousness' (Prefaced by Robin Ruiz, USA) and 'Refractions' (Prefaced by Alen Jacobs, U K) respectively. Dalip has been contributing his poems, reviews, criticisms, appraisals to various reputed national and international journals and magazines; e. zines and online publications are also daubed with his creative works some of which have also been anthologized. Laurels, commendation from newspapers and certificates and awards of excellence from India as well as from other countries like USA, UK, Canada, Italy, etc, for his creative writings speak volumes about him. Currently, he is also working as the editor of The Poetry Society of India (patronized by its Founder President, Dr. Madan Gandhi), as the editor of The Contemporary Literary Review of India, an international journal, and also as the co-editor of 'Contemporary Vibes', the refereed journal of literary criticism and creative writing.

Dolonchampa Chakraborty is a professional translator and editor. Worked for the Education Departments and city offices of USA, UK and Doctors Without Borders. A poet herself, she has two books of poetry to her credit. She was a panelist for the Bengali language in Indian Literary Festival, 2015. After managing the editorial responsibility of *Bookpocket*, an online Bengali magazine for three years, she is currently working as the editor of *The Nilgiri Wagon*, an online magazine in English that works to create a successful communication among the languages and literature of India and the rest of the world.

Don Martin is a best-selling author and editor who lives in Tucson, Arizona. His novels are usually classified as 'high-tech contemporary science fiction,' which he doesn't necessarily agree with, but he takes what he can gets. He also writes the widely-read column *The View From The Streets*, about issues homeless people face. Don is also a music writer and critic (concert and CD reviews, and band interviews) and a book reviewer. When not writing or editing you'll find him reading, mostly politics and history. But not science fiction! He doesn't much enjoy reading what he writes.

Duane Vorhees grew up in rural Ohio, in the US. After graduating from college he held a number of jobs, including lifeguard, carpenter, truck driver, dish washer, tool room attendant at a shipyard, door-to-door salesman, factory worker, and high school teacher, as he traveled extensively throughout North America. He was also involved in amateur theatricals and journalism. Eventually he went back to school and received a PhD in American Culture Studies from Bowling Green State University in Ohio and went to Korea to teach English at Seoul National University and other schools before joining the faculty of the University of Maryland University College, for whom he taught a number of classes in American Literature, American History, Government and Politics, Philosophy, Education, Library Science, and Sociology. He also became a charter member of SAN (Seoul Artists Network) and was an active participant at open mics. He has published academic papers, essays, and poems in numerous journals and is the author of *Loves I Bear To You* (2003). After retiring in 2014 he established duanespoetree.blogspot.com, a daily webzine that features creative contributions from artists of all stripes from around the world.

Dustin Pickering is founder of Transcendent Zero Press. Based in Houston, Texas, the press publishes an award nominated quarterly journal called *Harbinger Asylum*. He self-published two poetry collections, *The Daunting Ephemeral* and *The Future of Poetry is NOW: Bones Picking at Death's Howl*. Another poetry collection, *Salt and Sorrow*, was published by Chitrangi Publishers in 2016, and Hawakal Publishers took his collection of 'flash wisdom' titled *A Matter of Degrees*. Aside from being a poet and publisher, Pickering is an events coordinator in Houston, a visual artist, a songwriter, and an employee of Denson Home Health. He considers a life of study and writing to be his fate in life.

Eileen Register is author, teacher, and owner of The International Director of Published Authors.

Gopal Lahiri was born and grew up in Kolkata. He is an earth scientist by profession (passed out from Presidency College, Kolkata) and currently lives in Mumbai. He is a bilingual poet, writer, editor, critic and translator and widely published in Bengali and English language. He has five poetry collections in Bengali. His English poetry collections include *Silent Steps, Living Inside and Tidal Interlude*. and five POD books published from USA. Anthology appearances (among others) includes *National Treasures, Indus Valley, A Posy of Poesy, Concerto, Poet's paradise, My Dazzling Bards, The Silence within, East Lit, Indo-Australian Anthology, The Dance of the Peacock, Illuminations*. His works have featured in journals *Indian Literature, Taj Mahal Review, CLRI, Haiku Journal* and electronic publications *Arts and Letters, Eastlit, Grey Sparrow Journal, Dead Snake, Underground Window, Muse

India, Poetry Stop, Setu, Debug. He has jointly edited the anthology *Scaling Heights*. He was awarded *Poet of the Year, 2015* by Destiny Poets' International Community of Poets, *Wakefield, U.K.*

Kaushik Acharya is a high-school Sanskrit teacher and pursuing doctoral research [PhD] in Sanskrit Literature in Jadavpur University, Calcutta. He is the author of *Mumuksha* [Hawakal Publishers, Calcutta 2016], a book written in Sanskrit, which is the Sanskrit adaptation of Kiriti Sengupta's much acclaimed *Reflections on Salvation*. Acharya's several papers and articles have been published both in India and abroad.

Koushik Sen is a post-graduate student of English Literature in the University of Calcutta. His works have been published in *Harbinger Asylum*, *NY Literary Magazine*, *The Statesman*, *Lost Coast Review*, among other places. He is an avid book reader and loves to write a review only when he feels like writing for a book.

Manu S Kurup is a poet by passion and a teacher by profession. He has a PhD titled *The Art of Trouble: Popular Culture, Political Cartoons and Translation* from University of Hyderabad. A lifelong student of literature and culture, Manu has been writing poems since he was 13. He enjoys reading fantasy fiction and books onsocio-political issues. Though his profession requires him to teach Technical English to vibrant youngsters, he focuses more on bringing out their creative talent.

Munshi Md.Younus is the associate professor in the department of Bengali at Zakir Hussain Delhi College (Evening), Delhi University, India. He is the author of much acclaimed Bengali poetry book, *Nakshatra Barta* (Shambhabi Imprint 2017).

Nathan Hassall is an editor for *The Luxembourg Review* and co-founder and editor of experimental literary magazine, *Guttural*. He is an MA student in Creative Writing [Poetry] at the University of Kent and the author of *The Flesh and Mortar Prophecy* and *Of Gods and Gallows*.

Pranab Ghosh is a journalist, blogger and poet. His poems have been published in *Tuck Magazine*, *Dissident Voice*, *Literature Studio Review* and *Scarlet Leaf Review*, among other places. He has co-authored a book of poems, *Air & Age*. He has also translated a book of Bengali short stories into English, under the title *Bougainvillea and Other Stories* by Bitan Chakraborty.

P C K Prem is an author of more than fifty books. He has brought out ten volumes of poetry besides five books on criticism, two books on ancient literature, two on folktales, six novels and two collections of short fiction. His creative writings in Hindi include twenty novels, nine books on short fiction and a collection of poems. A winner of several prestigious awards, he is a poet, novelist, short story writer and a critic in English and Hindi from Himachal, India.

Rumpa Das is Deputy Secretary (Academic), West Bengal Board of Secondary Education. An alumnus of Jadavpur University, she was previously working as Associate Professor & Head, Department of English, Maheshtala College, near Batanagar. In her college, she was Coordinator for NAAC, and Programme Officer for NSS activities. Dr Das has written and edited five books, has published over forty-five articles in international and national books and journals and has spoken in over thirty academic conferences and seminars. Her areas of interest are Women's Studies, Media & Culture Studies, and ICT in Indian classrooms.

Saktipada Patra is the former Hornby Scholar of the British Council and he is presently the Resource Person of Oxford University Press and different colleges and universities in India.

Scott Thomas Outlar hosts the site 17 Numa. wordpress.com where links to his published poetry, fiction, essays, interviews, reviews, and books can be found. His work has appeared in hundreds of literary publications, both in the United States and internationally, and has been nominated for Best of the Next and the Pushcart Prize. Scott serves as an editor for *Walking Is Still Honest* Press, *The Blue Mountain Review*, *The Peregrine Muse*, and *Novelmasters*. His most recent poetry collection, *Happy Hour Hallelujah*, is available through CTU Publishing.

Seshu Chamarty has to his credit many articles published in the *New Indian Express* on Op-ed page. His poems appeared in some of the anthologies in UK and the US. His Haiku and Senryu found place or accepted for publication in prestigious online journals such as *World Haiku Review* and *Shamrock Haiku Journal*. He contributes to 'Citizen Speak' at msn.com (India) on various topics and is one of the top contributors. He was an officer with Andhra Bank for about twenty-five years. For some time he was practicing law in the High Court of Andhra Pradesh before he took up the job of an educationalist with a University. He had represented India at a literary festival in Jordon where he presented his poems in a University in Amman.

Sharmila Ray went to Presidency College and Calcutta University where she majored in History, did her Ph.D. on Durga and governance and subsequently joined City College, Kolkata under Calcutta University where she is now an Associate Professor and Head of the Department of History. She writes in English and has authored seven books of poetry, most recently *Scrawls and Scribbles* (Hawakal Publishers, Calcutta 2016). She has experimented her poems with Sarod (Indian string instrument) and the result is a CD— *Journey Through Poetry And Music*. Her poems are available in a CD- *Hello*. Her poems, short stories and non-fictional essays have appeared in various national and international magazines and journals.

To **Shernaz Wadia**, reading and writing poems has been one of the means to embark on an inward journey. She hopes her words will bring peace, hope and light into dark corners. Her poems have been published in many e-journals and anthologies. Wadia has published her own book of poems *Whispers of the Soul* and another titled *Tapestry Poetry — a Fusion of Two Minds* with her poetry partner Avril Meallem. Another volume of Tapestry Poetry is in the offing. Currently she is a columnist for *Different Truths*, a global participatory social journalism platform.

Soumen Jana is currently doing his doctoral research on Indian Theatre, especially on Badal Sircar. In the year 2012, he has had his Masters from Vidyasagar

University, Medinipur, West Bengal (India). He has also worked as a project assistant in a UGC-Sponsored MRP on Bengali Dalit Literature, conducted by the Department of English, Pondicherry University. He sometimes dabbles in translation, creative writing including Poetry and book reviews, and also some academic research papers.

Mumbai-based, **Sunil Sharma**, a college principal, is also widely-published Indian critic, poet, literary interviewer, editor, translator, essayist and fiction writer. He has published three collections of poetry, one collection of short fiction, one novel and co-edited six books so far. His six short stories and the novel Minotaurwere recently prescribed for the undergraduate classes under the Post-colonial Studies, Clayton University, Georgia, U.S.A. He is a recipient of the UK-based Destiny Poets' inaugural Poet of the Year award—2012. Recently his poems were published in the UN project: Happiness: The Delight-Tree. An English teacher with more than 23 years of degree-college teaching experience that includes administrative one (as vice-principal and now as full-fledged principal); freelance journalist with 15 years of experience writing for the supplements of the *Times of India*, Mumbai, India.

Born and brought up at Rasidpur village of Birbhum District, **Susanta Kumar Bardhan** graduated from Suri Vidyasagar College and did his M.A. in English from The University of Burdwan. He pursued his further study at Central Institute of English and Foreign Languages (CIEFL), Hyderabad [presently The English and Foreign Languages University (EFLU)] and completed Post Graduate Diploma in the Teaching of English (PGDTE), M. Phil (L & P) and Ph. D. (L & P) in English. Dr. Bardhan started his teaching career at Kamalanagar College, Mizoram and presently he is teaching English language and literature at Suri Vidyasagar College. He is associated with EFLU as a member of its External Faculty. His areas of interest are Linguistics, ELT, Stylistics and Modern British & Indian English Literature. Dr. Bardhan has published more than fifty research papers in the fields of Linguistics, ELT and English Literature in the leading national and international journals and books and presented more than thirty-five papers in several National and International Seminars. He has authored three books and edited three books. He did his post-PhD research during 2010-2013 as an Associate in UGC IUC for Higher Research in Humanities, Indian Institute of Advanced Study (IIAS), Shimla.

Tuhin Sanyal is an Assistant Professor in English at Tufanganj College in Cooch-Behar, West Bengal. Apart from an academic award from Berhampore University (Odisha) and the numerous academic papers and critical writings to his credit, he has penned three books of poems titled *White, Blue and Other Poems* (2004) archived in the National Library, *Phoenix on a Female Body and Other Poems* (2009), both published by Writers Workshop, Calcutta, and *The Nectar-Nook* (2016), which is an English rendering of Harivansh Rai Bachchan's *Madhushala*, published by Chitrangi, Kolkata.

Indian born **Usha Kishore** is a poet, editor and translator from the Sanskrit, resident on the Isle of Man, where she teaches English at Queen Elizabeth II High School. Kishore is internationally published and anthologised by *Macmillan, Hodder Wayland, Oxford University Press* (all UK) and *Harper Collins India* among others. Her poetry has won prizes in UK Poetry competitions, has been part of international projects and features in the British Primary and Indian Middle School and Undergraduate syllabi. The winner of an Arts Council Award and a *Culture Vannin* Award, Kishore's debut collection *On Manannan's Isle* was published in 2014 by *dpdotcom,* UK. A second collection, *Night Sky between the Stars (Cyberwit India)* and a book of translation from the Sanskrit, *Translations of the Divine Woman (Rasala India)*, have been published in 2015. Usha recently edited *Home Thoughts: Poetry of the British Indian Diaspora (Cyberwit India,* Jan 2017), with the Calcutta poet, academic and editor Jaydeep Sarangi. A third poetry collection is forthcoming in 2018.

Though **Vibha Malhotra** has been writing since she was seven, she took her "hobby" to the next level fairly recently. In 2010, she quit her well-paying job as a Senior Software Engineer at Adobe and during this break she completed a Master in Creative Writing from Newcastle University (UK). Apart from this Vibha became a published book reviewer, interviewer, poet, and editor. In 2012, She started a literary venture Literature Studio, through which she taught creative writing to aspiring writers. As an interviewer, she has interviewed historian and writer William Dalrymple, renowned authors Jerry Pinto and Jeet Thayil, and accomplished poet Sudeep Sen. Her works have been published in both local and international publications, such as *Wasafiri, Muse India,*

Tipton Poetry Journal, The Luxembourg Review, The Times of India, Ceylon Today, Red Fez, and *Dhaka Tribune.* Vibha has edited more than twenty books so far –*The Olive Picker: A Memoir* by Kathryn Brettell, *Queen Elizabeth II and the Royal Family, All About Everything, The Train Book, Hot Bikes,* and *Cool Cars* are just some of them. Currently, she is the editor-in-chief of the literary e-journal *Literature Studio Review. Know Your Worth,* a motivational book that she co-authored, has recently been published by General Press and is receiving rave reviews.

www.ingramcontent.com/pod-product-compliance
Lightning Source LLC
Chambersburg PA
CBHW021429080526
44588CB00009B/472